Resources for church leaders:

Biblical and pastoral responses to homosexuality

Edited by
Andrew Goddard and Don Horrocks

evangelical alliance
better together

Resources for church leaders:
Biblical and pastoral responses to homosexuality

©2012 Evangelical Alliance
ISBN 978-0-9572448-0-1

Whitefield House,
186 Kennington
Park Road,
London,
SE11 4BT

A company limited by guarantee Registered in England & Wales
No. 123448.

Registered Charity No England and Wales: 212325, Scotland: SC040576.

www.eauk.org

Acknowledgments

The Evangelical Alliance is grateful to the many people who, drawing on a wide range of scholarly expertise and pastoral experience, have helped shape this document. The initial work was carried out by an eight-member commission, one of whose members, the Rev Dr Andrew Goddard, produced a draft. Following comments from commission members, a revised text was unanimously agreed by commission members and sent to more than 40 readers for peer review. In the light of many helpful comments received from them, Dr Goddard and Dr Don Horrocks have finalised this published text.

Disclaimer

All the scenarios provided in this resource seek to be realistic but they are, of course, fictional constructions for reflection. Any similarity in content or names to any real situation is purely co-incidental.

Contents

Preface

It is now fourteen years since the Evangelical Alliance produced *Faith, Hope and Homosexuality*. That report was groundbreaking in various respects. It combined a clear and succinct statement of biblical teaching on marriage and sexuality with expressions of regret for the Church's past and present failings in relation to lesbians and gay men. It has served evangelicals and the wider church well, being extensively used as a valuable resource and position paper.

Over recent years, however, *Faith, Hope and Homosexuality* has become dated in the light of ongoing developments and discussions in church, academy and society. It has also become increasingly clear that many evangelicals are looking to the Evangelical Alliance for further guidance as to how its biblical stance would work out pastorally. With this in mind, it was decided not merely to revise the original report but to produce a new document with a practical, pastoral focus.

This new study and resource endorses and builds on the affirmations and recommendations of the original report. It has updated and reworded them where necessary to provide 10 affirmations re-stating the Evangelical Alliance's position. It reaffirms an evangelical sexual ethic, setting its discussion of homosexuality within the context of the gospel of grace and Christian teaching about love, marriage and sex more generally.

Like its predecessor, this document offers a fresh and positive contribution to ongoing debates. It engages realistically and honestly with real-life scenarios to help Christians, especially pastors and others in Christian ministry, discern how we can speak and live the truth in love.

We hope and pray that it will prove to be a practical resource for many years to come and enable evangelical churches and Christians to become more faithful and Christ-like witnesses to God's grace and truth.

Steve Clifford
General Director, Evangelical Alliance

Introduction

In 1998, the Evangelical Alliance's Commission on Unity and Truth among Evangelicals (ACUTE) produced *Faith, Hope and Homosexuality (FHH)*.[1] This report was well-received at the time as a significant contribution to the discussion. It gained the support of 96 per cent of Evangelical Alliance members[2] and has remained a valuable resource in the continuing debates on the subject among Christians. Why, then, produce yet another publication on the same subject?

For a number of years, the Evangelical Alliance and its Theology and Public Policy Advisory Commission (TAPPAC, the successor to ACUTE) have been aware of the need to revisit and review developments in this area since the publication of *FHH*. In 2010-11, an expert commission was established to undertake this work. It identified four key areas which explain why a new publication was thought to be desirable. These four areas have in turn helped to provide a shape and focus to what follows.

Changed context

First, the *context* today at the start of the second decade of the 21st century is different from that which the Evangelical Alliance addressed as we approached the new millennium. In the 14 years since *FHH* appeared, there have been significant social and legal changes in the United Kingdom and many other countries in relation to same-sex relationships. We have seen, for example, the equalization of the age of consent (from 2001 in England, Scotland and Wales and from 2008/9

---

[1] Evangelical Alliance's Commission on Unity and Truth among Evangelicals (ACUTE) 1998. This is referred to as *FHH* throughout this publication. It can be obtained as an e-document on request to the Evangelical Alliance.

[2] The Evangelical Alliance survey for the 1996 Assembly of Evangelicals found that 96 per cent of Evangelical Alliance member churches thought homosexual activity to be wrong.

in Northern Ireland), the introduction of civil partnerships (under the Civil Partnership Act 2004) and the inclusion of sexual orientation within much equality legislation. Most recently, the Prime Minister signalled his support for legislation to redefine marriage to include same-sex couples and consultation on this proposal began in March 2012. The Evangelical Alliance is part of widespread popular opposition to these proposals on the basis that no group or government should be able to redefine marriage which, as the fundamental basis of human society, is uniquely between one man and one woman.

More widely, gay and lesbian people and their relationships are now much more accepted in British society (although there is still more uncertainty or unhappiness about social changes in this area than some realise[3]). They are also much more visible in our churches, including many evangelical churches. This also means that, in contrast to the 1990s, most evangelical Christians are now aware that they have gay and lesbian friends, family members, neighbours or work colleagues. As a result, many more Christians' reflections and responses in relation to this subject are framed by direct personal experience as well as reading of Scripture or acceptance of traditional evangelical teaching.

Despite this significant and fairly rapid cultural change, the situation in the Christian church has remained relatively constant. Across a number of denominations, the opening words of Joel Edwards, then General Director of the Evangelical Alliance, in his Foreword to *FHH* are probably still true –

---

[3]   *FHH* claimed "more than two-thirds of men and more than half of women in Britain still believe homosexual practice to be essentially wrong", noting that "this must be set against a general decline in disapproval since the 1960s" (FHH, p. 1). In January 2010, however, the 26th Report of British Social Attitudes found that in 2008 just over a third of people (36 per cent) thought sexual relations between two adults of the same sex were 'always' or 'mostly' wrong, whereas nearly two-thirds (62 per cent) had thought this in 1983. In 2008, 39 per cent of people thought same-sex sexual relations were "not wrong at all". See http://www.natcen.ac.uk/media-centre/press-releases/2010-press-releases/british-social-attitudes-26th-report--britain-becoming-increasingly-liberal

"Homosexuality may well be the single most divisive issue in the Western Church today."[4] Evangelicals continue to be involved in discussions in various churches. They remain among the clearest advocates for upholding the traditional Christian and biblical vision of human sexuality set out in *FHH*. In the Evangelical Alliance's survey of 21st century evangelicals, only 16 per cent of respondents from festivals and churches expressed disagreement with the strong statement that "homosexual actions are always wrong" while 59 per cent agreed with it "a lot".[5]

Need for pastoral guidance

Second, especially in the light of these cultural changes, an increasing concern has been the need for more practical and pastoral advice for evangelicals, particularly church leaders, in this area. *FHH*, in its report and recommendations, gave a number of pointers as to the shape of a faithful, gracious Christian response to those who experience same-sex attraction. This area was, however, under-developed in *FHH* compared to its more wide-ranging treatment of such matters as the witness of Scripture, science and history. Given increasing numbers of requests for guidance from Evangelical Alliance members and church leaders, it was therefore felt that there was an urgent need for more pastoral guidance. This is the major new contribution in this publication.

---

[4] Most recently the presbyterian Church of Scotland has acknowledged its divisions on the subject. See http://www.churchofscotland.org.uk/__data/assets/pdf_file/0006/5757/ga11_specssrm.pdf for its report. It has already seen a number of evangelical ministers and churches announce they will leave as a result of decisions at its May 2011 General Assembly.

[5] Evangelical Alliance 2011b, p. 9. Within evangelical churches in the sample there was even stronger support – only 10 per cent expressed disagreement and 68 per cent agreed "a lot" (Evangelical Alliance 2011a, p. 24, Table 6.8).

Ongoing discussion

Third, the *literature* on the subject has continued to expand in a wide range of areas, both biblical and theological and in relation to science and society. A number of major works have appeared from evangelicals and others. Although evangelicals need to become aware of these and can benefit from them, it is not possible for most church leaders to keep up reading and thinking in this complex area. This resource therefore seeks to summarise some of the major developments and, in its notes, bibliography and guide to further reading, to provide an accessible way into the wider recent literature.

Consistent content

Fourth, it was agreed that the *content* of *FHH* remained of value and that any new publication should build upon and develop it rather than significantly revise it when addressing pastoral issues. Thus, not all areas covered in *FHH* are revisited here. However, because evangelicalism is marked by a commitment to "the divine inspiration and supreme authority of the Old and New Testament Scriptures, which are the written Word of God – fully trustworthy for faith and conduct",[6] the crucial area of Scripture's teaching is again discussed in some detail.

The fundamental continuity with *FHH* is signalled by the 10 affirmations which shape both the structure and substance of this new publication. These restate (although restructured and to varying degrees reworded) and reaffirm as its current position the original meaning and substance of the twelve concluding affirmations and recommendations of *FHH* which defined the Evangelical Alliance's position on homosexuality and were approved by the Evangelical Alliance Council in 1998.

---

6   This is the second point in the Evangelical Alliance's Basis of Faith which can be found at http://www.eauk.org/about/basis-of-faith.cfm

A guide to this resource

The five chapters of this resource are structured around the 10 affirmations which follow this introduction. Each chapter opens with one or more of these affirmations, which are then explored and expounded in the chapter.

Chapter One is based on the first foundational affirmation. It clarifies what is under discussion in considering homosexuality, while setting the discussion in the context of the Christian gospel and an evangelical ethos. **Chapter Two** then provides the biblical and theological basis for two affirmations which set out the principles for pastoral practice. It sets the discussion of homosexuality within a wider biblical sexual ethic whose framework is focussed on marriage and other forms of loving human relationships. It also examines the biblical texts which address same-sex sexual behaviour. The chapter also affirms God's love and concern for all and acknowledges the Church's failings in this area in relation to sexual minorities. With these theological principles and biblical exegesis and interpretation in place, attention is turned more specifically to pastoral practice.

Chapter Three develops a proposed framework for pastoral practice in relation to four affirmations concerning support for those who experience same-sex attraction and church policy in relation to ordination and blessings. The final two chapters then draw on all these affirmations to consider pastoral practice in much more detail. By means of nine fictional but realistic scenarios, reflections are offered on an illustrative range of practical issues in church life where we believe evangelicals would value more structured guidance. **Chapter Four** explores responses in relation to same-sex orientation and adds an eighth affirmation. **Chapter Five** seeks to describe how, in creating a community of grace and truth, evangelicals may respond to those involved in same-sex behaviour and relationships in a manner consistent with earlier affirmations and summarised in the final two affirmations. Finally, in addition to an extensive **Bibliography**, with a particular emphasis on works which have appeared since *FHH*'s publication, there is also a shorter guide for those interested in exploring **Further Reading**.

Affirmations

We are conscious that different evangelicals might apply certain of these points in different ways, but we believe that, taken together, they reflect an authentic, mainstream evangelical response to homosexuality in general and sexually active same-sex partnerships in particular:

1. We recognise that all of us are sinners, and that the only true hope for sinful people – whatever our sexuality – is in Jesus Christ. Our earnest prayer is that his love, truth and grace would characterise evangelical responses to debates on homosexuality, both now and in future.

2. We affirm God's love and concern for all human beings, whatever their sexuality, and so repudiate all attitudes and actions which victimise or diminish people whose affections are directed towards people of the same sex. We are encouraged many Christians now recognise and deeply regret the hurt caused by past and present failures in their responses to those who experience same-sex attraction.

3. We affirm that marriage is an institution created by God in which one man and one woman enter into an exclusive relationship for life. Marriage is the only form of partnership approved by God for sexual relations and homoerotic sexual practice is incompatible with His will as revealed in Scripture. We do not accept that holding these theological and ethical views on biblical grounds is in itself homophobic.

4. We encourage evangelical congregations to be communities of grace in which those who experience same-sex attraction and seek to live faithfully in accordance with biblical teaching are welcomed and affirmed. Such Christians need churches which are safe spaces where they are able to share and explore their stories with fellow believers for mutual encouragement and support as we help each other grow together into maturity in Christ.

5. We oppose moves within certain churches to accept and/or endorse sexually active same-sex partnerships as a legitimate form of Christian relationship and to permit the ordination to ministry of those in such sexual relationships. We stand prayerfully with those in such churches who are seeking to resist these moves on biblical grounds.

6. We oppose church services of blessing for civil partnerships and other forms of gay and lesbian relationships as unbiblical and reject any redefinition of marriage to encompass same-sex relationships.

7. We commend and encourage all those who experience same-sex attraction and have committed themselves to chastity by refraining from homoerotic sexual practice. We believe they should be eligible for ordination and leadership within the church, recognising that they can bring invaluable insights and experience to the sphere of Christian pastoral ministry.

8. We welcome and support the work of those individuals and organisations who responsibly seek to help Christians who experience same-sex attraction as in conflict with their commitment to live in accordance with biblical teaching. This help will involve counsel and pastoral support to live a chaste life and, as part of this process, some may seek and experience changes in the strength or direction of their same-sex attractions

9. We believe both habitual homoerotic sexual activity without repentance and public promotion of such activity are inconsistent with faithful church membership. While processes of membership and discipline differ from one church context to another, we believe that either of these behaviours warrants consideration for church discipline.

10. We encourage evangelical congregations to welcome and accept sexually active lesbians and gay men. However, they should do so in the expectation that they, like all of us who are living outside God's purposes, will come in due course to see the need to be transformed and live in accordance with biblical revelation and orthodox church teaching. We urge gentleness, patience and ongoing pastoral care during this process and after a person renounces same-sex sexual relations.

Chapter One
Homosexuality and the Gospel: An Evangelical Approach

Affirmation
(1) We recognise that all of us are sinners, and that the only true hope for sinful people – whatever our sexuality – is in Jesus Christ. Our earnest prayer is that his love, truth and grace would characterise evangelical responses to debates on homosexuality, both now and in future.

In any area – particularly such contested and painful areas as sexual ethics and the appropriate pastoral response to gay and lesbian Christians – it is vital evangelicals begin with the gospel and let it shape both *what* we say and *how* we say it. This first affirmation helpfully summarises a number of central points which can easily get lost in both internal church discussions about sexuality and in how Christians speak and are heard when they address these issues within wider society.

1.1 Our common humanity: "all of us are sinners" and "the only true hope... is in Jesus Christ"

One of the fundamental problems of much Christian consideration of homosexuality is that it can implicitly – or even explicitly – single out and focus attention on those people who experience same-sex attraction. Their lives can then be subject to intense scrutiny and the passing of moral judgments by those who often have little or no personal knowledge of what it means to be attracted to someone of the same sex or be tempted by homosexual sin. This differentiation between 'us' and 'them' is particularly ironic given that the fullest biblical discussion of the subject is Romans 1 where "Paul's *primary* concern [...] is not homoerotic sexual practice, but the more fundamental sin of refusing to glorify and give thanks to God" (v.21).[7] Indeed, his analysis of homosexuality is offered as part of an argument whose climax – often lost because of our chapter breaks – is "You, therefore, have no excuse, you who pass judgment on someone else, for at whatever point you judge another, you are condemning yourself, because you who pass judgment do the same things" (Rom. 2.1). This stark challenge then leads to the conclusion of his argument towards the end of the next chapter that "all have sinned and fall short of the glory of God" (Rom. 3.23).

Evangelical theology has always had a realistic and robust doctrine of both the goodness of creation and the universality of our sinful condition making us all equally subject to God's condemnation. Thus the Evangelical Alliance's doctrinal basis affirms "The dignity of all people, made male and female in God's image to love, be holy and care for creation, yet corrupted by sin, which incurs divine wrath and judgement."[8] This stands as a reminder that any identification of particular acts as sins and any pastoral response to those who struggle with or succumb to temptation in this area can only be the humble and penitent action of those who know themselves to be fellow sinners.

We must also approach all questions in this area on the basis that, in the words of this first affirmation, "the only true hope for sinful people – whatever our sexuality – is in Jesus Christ." All of us are called to a life of holiness but it is not our faithful obedience or our conformity to a sexual ethic, much less being or becoming heterosexual, which is offered as the basis for hope. All of us always remain sinners and our only true hope is in Christ, our union with him through new birth, faith and baptism and his promise to make us and all things new.

The good news of this common shared hope is particularly important for those Christians whose lives are marked by struggling with same-sex

---

7 *FHH*, p. 18.

8 This is the fourth point in the Basis of Faith which can be found at
   http://www.eauk.org/about/basis-of-faith.cfm

attraction. Their testimonies of what it means to be living in hope are one of the gifts they offer and lessons they teach to the wider church as it struggles against temptation and sin. In one of the earliest evangelical writings about the reality of living with homosexuality, Alex Davidson, writes:

Isn't it one of the most wretched things about this condition that when you look ahead, the same impossible road seems to continue indefinitely? You're driven to rebellion when you think of there being no point in it and to despair when you think of there being no limit to it. That's why I find a comfort, when I feel desperate, or rebellious, or both, to remind myself of God's promise that one day it will be finished. [9]

In a similar and more recent powerful testimony, Wesley Hill reflects on Christian faithfulness and homosexuality under the title *Washed and Waiting.* Quoting Romans 8, he writes:

So much of my life as a homosexual Christian... has simply been learning how to wait, to be patient, to endure, to bear up under an unwelcome burden for the long haul.... Washed and waiting. That is my life – my identity as one who is forgiven and spiritually cleansed and my struggle as one who perseveres with a frustrating thorn in the flesh, looking forward to what God has promised to do. [10]

1.2 The gospel as good news for all

By beginning with our solidarity alongside all humanity in Adam and the universal offer of salvation in Christ, this opening affirmation also reminds us of the need to consider how an evangelical response to homosexuality is faithful to and supportive of our primary call to evangelism and sharing

---

9   Davidson 1970, p. 85 quoted in Stott 1998, p. 45.

10   Hill 2010, p. 50.

in God's mission: how can the church offer – and be seen and heard to offer – good news to all, including those who identify as gay and lesbian?

Jesus' pattern of ministry in the gospels combines the clear and rigorous demands of discipleship with a welcome of sinners that was so attractive to them and so wide and inclusive that it caused scandal among the religious leaders of God's people concerned to protect Israel's purity. As evangelicals seeking to present Christ credibly as good news for spiritual and social transformation we need to uphold God's standards in the public square and in our churches when they are challenged and undermined. We must, however, take care to do this in such a way that does not obscure our central message that "the only true hope for sinful people – whatever our sexuality – is in Jesus Christ."

As gay and lesbian people have become more publicly visible and accepted, many evangelicals have discovered them among their friends but struggled to know how to share the gospel with them. The difficulty here can be deepened when evangelical Christians are viewed in a negative light because of their ethical and political stance in relation to homosexuality. This is much more of a challenge today than in the past and, if taken seriously, it will inevitably generate new pastoral questions some of which are discussed in chapters four and five.[11]

1.3 The problems with labels

In emphasising that we are all sinners whose only hope is in Christ, the affirmation states that this is true "whatever our sexuality". By refocusing us on our common humanity, this helpfully provides a theological basis for

---

11 Although aspects of his ministry and writing have been challenged by some evangelicals, Andrew Marin offers one pattern of how it is possible to build bridges and develop relationships as Christians with the gay and lesbian community without needing first to accept revisionist positions on sexual ethics. See Marin 2009a and the interview with him at Marin 2009b.

challenging and relativising the common pattern of classifying, identifying and distinguishing ourselves on the basis of our sexual 'orientation' and in particular the regular labels of 'homosexual' and 'heterosexual'. The binary model of two fixed and enduring categories of human sexual desire – for the same sex (homosexual) and for the opposite sex (heterosexual) – is flawed both theologically and in relation to the scientific and psychological evidence concerning human sexuality. [12]

1.3.1 Theological challenges

Theologically, one of the best explorations of this remains the St. Andrew's Day Statement produced by a group of theologians for the Church of England Evangelical Council in 1995. It opens with three theological principles within a Trinitarian structure. Its first, Christological principle includes the statement that:

In him [Jesus Christ] we know both God and human nature as they truly are. In his life, death and resurrection we are adopted as children of God and called to follow in the way of the cross. His promise and his call are for every human being: that we should trust in him, abandon every self-justification, and rejoice in the good news of our redemption.

This is then applied and expounded in relation to how we should understand ourselves and our sexuality:

Our sexual affections can no more define who we are than can our class, race or nationality. At the deepest ontological level, therefore, there is no such thing as 'a' homosexual or 'a' heterosexual; there are human beings, male and female, called to redeemed humanity in Christ, endowed with a complex variety of emotional potentialities and threatened by a complex variety of forms of alienation.[13]

---

12 *FHH* was, in places, too uncritical of this distinction, dividing people into "homosexual and heterosexual".

13 The statement appears in various places, perhaps most accessibly in the book produced with reactions to it – Bradshaw 2003, pp. 5-11 (here at p. 6 and then p. 7).

1.3.2 Scientific challenges

In terms of scientific and psychological evidence, research into the complex reality of human sexuality supports this theological critique of any belief that the pattern of our sexual affections is woven into our being "at the deepest ontological level". The binary model, where our sexuality is viewed like a switch which is set either to 'homosexual' or 'heterosexual', continues to shape much popular and even legal thinking. It is, however, now generally agreed that it is best to understand human sexual attraction in terms of a spectrum. In the words of psychiatrist Professor Glynn Harrison:

> the idea that sexual 'orientation' exists in fixed and unalterable categories has been the subject of increasing criticism in recent decades. Objections have been raised from a diverse range of theoretical perspectives, including labelling theory, life-course developmental theory and evolutionary psychology. [14]

As far back as the late 1940s, the Kinsey scale was adopted which offers a seven-point scale ranging from exclusively heterosexual (0) through to exclusively homosexual (6) with various weightings between these two poles (1-5). This has been used, adapted and extended in various ways by subsequent researchers.[15]

This question of how we conceptualise sexuality and homosexuality within this is an important issue in relation to a number of areas. One of these – the question of a person possibly seeking to change their sexual attractions – is explored further in chapter four (especially 4.2.2), but another is the regularly asked question of prevalence – what proportion of the population are homosexual?

---

14 Harrison 2008, p. 297.

15 A helpful guide to this whole debate is Stein 1999 with chapter 2 particularly focussed on this question.

1.4 Sexual minorities

1.4.1 Questions of names and numbers

In relation to prevalence, there are a range of important prior questions that will influence the final figures. Data in this area are likely to vary depending on such factors as survey methods, populations, and the concept and labels of 'orientation' or 'identity' used. The two most important factors are how 'homosexual' is defined in any survey and the reliability of the methods used in the survey. For example, a study of Australian twins in 2000 found that for each man identifying as completely homosexual (Kinsey scale 6, 2 per cent) there were three times as many who identified some degree of homosexual feeling (Kinsey scale 1-5, 6 per cent). The importance of using the spectrum model was even more evident in a finding (confirmed by other studies) which highlights the need to distinguish male and female sexuality: only around 0.5 per cent of women identified as completely homosexual (Kinsey scale 6) but 8 per cent of women reported slight, substantial or predominantly homosexual feelings.[16]

In the UK, the most recent data is that supplied in 2010 by the Office of National Statistics (ONS) from a large sample of nearly quarter of a million people in the Integrated Household Survey questioned between April 2009 and March 2010.[17] This examined sexual self-identity and positioned itself between a simple binary model of "gay or straight?" and the more developed spectrum found in Kinsey. It asked respondents over 16 which of four possible terms best described how they thought of themselves. The results were:[18]

---

16 Bailey, Dunne, and Martin 2000.

17 Joloza et al. 2010. This report can be downloaded from http://www.ons.gov.uk/ons/guide-method/measuring-equality/equality/sexual-identity-project/measuring-sexual-identity--an-evaluation-report.pdf

18 These do not total 100 per cent because 3.2 per cent refused to answer or said "don't know" and no data was recorded for 0.6 per cent of the sample.

"Heterosexual or Straight"   94.2 per cent

"Gay or Lesbian"   0.9 per cent

"Bisexual"   0.5 per cent

"Other"   0.5 per cent[19]

Prevalence figures across various studies have appeared in the range of 1 per cent to 8 per cent. While noting that higher figures are commonly used as estimates, the ONS compared its findings with other UK surveys of the LGB (Lesbian, Gay, and Bisexual) population. It concluded that the "estimate of 1.4 per cent LGB is broadly consistent with other household surveys in the UK that asked questions about sexual identity. This is also consistent with previous research which found survey estimates range between 0.3 per cent and 3.0 per cent."[20] On these figures, there would be about 466,000 adults over 16 in the UK who identify as gay or lesbian and just under 230,000 who identify as bisexual.[21]

---

19 The report notes that this "other" category "was included to address the fact that not all people will fall in the first three categories and that some people such as those that are asexual, may feel no sense of sexual identity at all. In addition, individuals who disagree with the simplistic male/female gender binary, or who were against categorisation based on the gender of people to whom they were attracted or with whom they had relations, could also prefer to identify as other. Previous ONS work also showed that a small number of heterosexual respondents may not understand the terminology used in the question so may select 'Other' instead" (p. 11).

20 Joloza et al. 2010, p. 15. An April 2011 report in the US found that 1.8 per cent of adults in the US identified as bisexual and 1.7 per cent as lesbian or gay (Gates 2011). Despite this, a May 2011 survey by Gallup reported that "U.S. adults, on average, estimate that 25 per cent of Americans are gay or lesbian. More specifically, over half of Americans (52 per cent) estimate that at least one in five Americans are gay or lesbian, including 35 per cent who estimate that more than one in four are in this category. Thirty percent put the figure at less than 15 per cent." See report at http://www.gallup.com/poll/147824/Adults-Estimate-Americans-Gay-Lesbian.aspx.

21 For a short summary of the most recent evidence from the US in relation to sexuality, especially bisexuality, see Goddard and Harrison 2011a.

1.4.2 LGB people in the UK

Because of the large sample the data could be broken down and examined in a number of areas. This produced the following findings which give an insight into the British LGB population:

- Among those who identified as "bisexual", two-thirds were women whereas among those who chose 'gay or lesbian', 68 per cent were men and 32 per cent were women. Overall, slightly more women identified as 'bisexual' than 'lesbian' and this confirms the evidence noted above concerning women's greater diversity across the spectrum of sexuality.

- Among those identifying as LGB, 63 per cent were single (though many of these were cohabiting). However, 16 per cent were married and living with a spouse, 1 per cent married but separated, 6 per cent divorced and 1 per cent widowed. Only 12 per cent were currently or previously in a civil partnership. Thus nearly a quarter of those identifying as gay, lesbian or bisexual were married or had been married, roughly twice as many as were or had been in a same-sex civil partnership.

- Living with a partner, but outside marriage or a civil partnership, was more common among LGB respondents than heterosexuals. Forty-three per cent of those identifying as LGB who were not married and living with their spouse or in a current civil partnership lived as part of a couple. This was just over 30 per cent of all LGB respondents, over twice as many as in a civil partnership. In contrast, only 34 per cent of heterosexual respondents who were not married and living with their spouse lived as part of a cohabiting couple. This was 18 per cent of all straight respondents, well under half the number who are married.

- Just over a third (34.5 per cent) of LGB respondents said they had no religion compared to only a fifth (20.5 per cent) of those identifying as heterosexual/straight.

- Those who identified as LGB had a younger age profile. Almost two-thirds (65.7 per cent) were under 45 whereas less than half (48.5 per cent) of those who identified as heterosexual were in this age range. Among those 65 and over, slightly more of those identifying as LGB identified as bisexual than gay or lesbian. This signals the social and other factors that impact how people respond to these questions.

- All regions of the UK had between 0.9 per cent and 1.5 per cent identifying as LGB except for two: the South West had 1.6 per cent of the population and London had the largest proportion of adults identifying as LGB at 2.2 per cent.

The format of this major survey points to two further important issues in considering labels – first, the basis on which (homo)sexuality is identified and classified (1.5) and, second, the terminology that should be used in discussing homosexuality today (1.6).

1.5 What we are talking about: Five categories

In defining its terms FHH drew heavily on the common distinction between what it called homosexual "orientation" and homosexual "practice".[22] Broadly speaking, the former relates to matters of personal self-discovery and self-description whereas the latter relates to choices as regards personal conduct, usually in the light of that self-discovery. This distinction remains crucially important, will be explored further in chapter three (see 3.1 below), and will shape our consideration of pastoral issues with chapter four focussed on 'orientation' and chapter five on 'practice'. However, the complexities of sexuality – particularly what FHH categorised under the single heading of 'orientation' – have become

---

22 *FHH*, pp. 5-6. This is similar to the ONS report's distinction between attraction and behaviour. Sexual attraction "refers to a sexual interest in another person based on a combination of factors" and can also be understood as "having sexual feelings towards someone". Sexual behaviour in contrast refers to "how people behave sexually" and, in relation to homosexuality, "whether they have sexual partners of the same sex or not" (Joloza et al. 2010, p. 6) which is broadly synonymous with what FHH referred to as homosexual (or homoerotic sexual) practice and defined as "genital or other activity pertaining to sexual arousal between people of the same sex" (FHH, p. 6).

clearer in recent years. Perhaps the most helpful categorisation in this area is that offered by evangelical psychology professor Mark Yarhouse. In his book, *Homosexuality and the Christian*, Yarhouse offers a three-fold distinction.[23]

Attraction

The first tier within "orientation" is that of "same-sex attraction" (often abbreviated to SSA). This is a description of feelings experienced and hence something which is generally out of a person's control. As Yarhouse comments:

> *Certain people, regardless of the cause, have experiences of attraction to the same sex. This fact doesn't say anything about either their identity or their behavior. It doesn't hint at who they are or what they do. It is descriptive. We are simply talking about the fact that a person experiences same-sex attraction.*[24]

Orientation

Secondly, there is sexual "orientation".[25] This is where the experience of attraction is such in terms of its strength, durability and persistence that a person feels oriented in a certain way, for example 'homosexual', 'heterosexual' or 'bisexual'. There is, of course, no scientific way of defining when sexual attractions amount to an orientation and this will be a subjective assessment based on each person's own experience of attraction.

---

23 Yarhouse 2010. This subject is introduced in chapter 2, especially pp. 41ff.

24 Yarhouse 2010, p. 41.

25 This use of the same term 'orientation' is more specific and precise than the broader sense of 'orientation' contrasted with 'practice'. Where important, it should be clear in what follows which of the two senses is intended.

Identity

Thirdly, there is what Yarhouse calls "gay identity".[26] This is the socio-cultural label that the ONS survey was seeking to measure and which it described in terms of how people think of themselves.[27] A person's sexual identity is often the culmination of a long process of identity formation as they seek to understand themselves – particularly their sexual attractions or orientation – in relation to other people and wider society. This process may lead simply to a private sexual identity but can culminate in "coming out" – a public declaration of one's perceived sexual identity. Such an identity is most marked in those who embrace it as part of a political campaign to attack what they see as heterosexism and homophobia. As it is a social construction, this identity is not only a relatively recent phenomenon but also one whose labels and distinctions are susceptible to change, particularly between generations.[28] It is this aspect of homosexuality which Yarhouse particularly focuses on, offering an alternative of identity formation in Christ to that of being gay or lesbian.

Practice: Behaviour and Relationship

This three-fold categorisation within "orientation" needs to be supplemented by a distinction within "practice". This is the distinction between *behaviour* – a person's sexual activity[29] – and *relationship*. All

---

26 Yarhouse 2010, pp. 42-3. Yarhouse here uses 'gay' generically to cover both 'gay' and 'lesbian' identities.

27 Joloza et al. 2010, p. 6. The report notes that identity does not necessarily match attraction or behaviour and can change over time and took the view that orientation could be derived from attraction, behaviour or identity.

28 Savin-Williams 2005. In this book a secular gay therapist and psychology professor explores the changing understandings and labels of sexual identity among American teenagers.

29 "Men who have sex with men" (MSM) is a purely behavioural category created by epidemiologists studying HIV/AIDS among men engaged in homosexual behaviour even if they rejected a gay identity.

of us have both same-sex and opposite-sex relationships and Christians recognise marriage as a specific pattern of opposite-sex relationship given by God in creation. Questions arise about how to understand, evaluate and respond to other special and distinctive but non-marital forms of relationships. In relation to homosexuality this particularly applies where someone has a central, defining, intimate relationship with someone of the same sex (for example, a civil partner).

Summary
There are thus five distinct categories which need to be considered if we are to understand (homo)sexuality:

- *Attraction* – our sexual feelings and interests
- *Orientation* – a perceived settled pattern to our sexual attractions[30]
- *Identity* – a label to identify ourselves in terms of our sexuality
- *Behaviour* – our sexual activity
- *Relationship* – a central, defining intimate relationship

The complex interaction of categories
Clearly these five different categories could, in a particular case, at a particular time, all point to what is traditionally understood as homosexuality – someone is so strongly same-sex attracted as to have a homosexual orientation and identify as 'gay' or 'lesbian' and they are in a sexually active civil partnership. There are, however, numerous other combinations. Someone could, for example in prison, engage in

---

30 In relation to prevalence in terms of attraction or orientation rather than identity, Harrison offers three conclusions: (1) "most men (c.85–90 per cent) and most women (c.70–80 per cent) report only ever having been attracted to members of the opposite sex"; (2) "a significant minority, 10–15 per cent of men and 20–30 per cent of women, experience same-sex desires at some time in their life"; (3) "a much smaller group, about 2.5 per cent of men and 1.75 per cent of women, understand themselves to be 'predominantly' same-sex attracted in terms of desire and behaviour" (Harrison 2008 p. 300).

homosexual behaviour while being married, identifying as heterosexual and having a heterosexual orientation with little or no experience of same-sex attraction. Alternatively, someone may have strong same-sex attractions and consider themselves same-sex oriented but reject the identity of 'gay' and live a celibate, single life or be faithful in their marriage.

1.6 Clarifying terms

This wide variety of scenarios and phenomena which can be included in thinking about homosexuality combines with different moral evaluations of it to make it difficult to find agreed and acceptable terminology. As *FHH* noted, "The actual word 'homosexuality' was first used only in 1869".[31] It is certainly not a biblical term and evangelicals should therefore not feel bound to it or to any other particular language in this discussion. In fact, 'homosexual' is best avoided, certainly as a noun, as it is considered pejorative and rejected by many people because of its association with a medical/scientific approach, social stigma and an oppressive attitude.[32] In common usage, 'gay' (in relation to men but sometimes generically) and 'lesbian' (in relation to women) are the preferred terms and these are often reduced to initials and combined with those for others who identify as sexual minorities.[33]

In what follows, 'homosexuality' will be retained as the best generic term for the whole area under discussion but (unless reporting or quoting others) 'homosexual' will not be used as a noun in relation to people but

---

31 *FHH*, p. 21.

32 Andrew Marin describes his realisation of the importance of this in communicating with the GLBT community at Marin 2009a, pp. 60-1.

33 Probably the most common label now is LGBT (Lesbian, Gay, Bisexual and Transgender) or GLBT but other letters eg Q for Queer or Questioning, I for Intersex, U for Unsure are sometimes added. For the Evangelical Alliance's discussion of Transgender issues see Evangelical Alliance Policy Commission 2000.

only as an adjective in relation to behaviour where it refers to what FHH called "homoerotic sexual practice". In relation to attraction, orientation and relationships the adjective 'same-sex' will generally be applied whereas people will be described as 'those who experience same-sex attraction (SSA)' or, where it is necessary to use common self-ascribed social identities, as 'gay', 'lesbian' or 'bisexual'.

1.7 The centrality of Christ's grace and truth

The final substantive paragraph of FHH reads:

> *In all aspects of the Christian life, and not least in relation to homosexuality, it is essential to balance biblical sexual morality with biblical grace in our response to every individual. Truth asserted without grace can often seem cold, condemning and occupied more with the letter than the spirit of the law. But the heart of the Gospel is that truth finds its fulfilment in God's grace, offering the chance of repentance, forgiveness, and new life. Such truth is not compromised when compassion and respect are shown to an individual; nor are such responses a seal of approval on wrong behaviour. They are, rather, a sign of God's love.* [34]

This is the basis for the opening affirmation's prayer that Christ's "love, truth and grace would characterise evangelical responses to debates on homosexuality, both now and in future". John's gospel opens with the good news that "The Word became flesh and made his dwelling among us. We have seen his glory, the glory of the one and only Son, who came from the Father, full of grace and truth... the law was given through Moses; grace and truth came through Jesus Christ" (John 1.14, 17).

The danger in much contemporary church life, particularly in relation to this subject, is that grace and truth are thought to be incompatible or at least are often not combined in practice. Evangelicals do not however

---

34 *FHH*, pp. 31-2.

separate the two. The following chapter seeks graciously to articulate the truth as it has been revealed in Scripture and received by the church. The third chapter then attempts to discern what it might mean to obey and live that truth in both word and deed so that in chapters four and five consideration can be given to the shape of a community of grace and truth that trusts that "Grace, mercy and peace from God the Father and from Jesus Christ, the Father's Son, will be with us in truth and love" (2 John v3).

Chapter Two

Truths to Live By

Affirmations

(2) We affirm God's love and concern for all human beings, whatever their sexuality, and so repudiate all attitudes and actions which victimise or diminish people whose affections are directed towards people of the same sex. We are encouraged many Christians now recognise and deeply regret the hurt caused by past and present failures in their responses to those who experience same-sex attraction.

(3) We affirm that marriage is an institution created by God in which one man and one woman enter into an exclusive relationship for life. Marriage is the only form of partnership approved by God for sexual relations and homoerotic sexual practice is incompatible with His will as revealed in Scripture. We do not accept that holding these theological and ethical views on biblical grounds is in itself homophobic.

Pastoral care must be shaped not only by love and grace but by the truth as God has revealed it to us in Scripture. In particular there are two key areas that need to be considered: an evangelical understanding of sexual ethics (2.1-2.3 below) and an understanding of the need for a loving Christian response to gay and lesbian people which rejects homophobia in the sense of wrong attitudes and actions towards them (2.4).[35]

---

35 Both 'homophobia' and 'homophobic' are terms which are often and increasingly used in a polemical way to dismiss, by means of a negative label, those holding traditional Christian views and thus effectively bring reasoned dialogue to an end. Although these terms are used in this resource, as noted in the third affirmation and discussed further below, this wide-ranging definition is rejected. Popular misuse of them shows it is important to use these words with clarity and care as to their meaning and rhetorical effect.

2.1 Sexual ethics and the Bible[36]

The third affirmation which heads this chapter sums up the evangelical understanding of a biblical sexual ethic and the question of homosexuality in relation to two areas:

1. Marriage is "an institution created by God in which one man and one woman enter into an exclusive relationship for life" and it is "the only form of partnership approved by God for sexual relations" and

2. "Homoerotic sexual practice" is "incompatible with His will as revealed in Scripture".

In terms of the five categories outlined in the previous chapter (1.5), these two convictions clearly relate to *practice* i.e. sexual *behaviour* and the proper *relationship* for full sexual relations. They do not address the questions of *attraction, orientation* or *identity*.

2.1.1 Love and four forms of loving relationship

Both of the two points summarised above offer a brief summary which derives from a wider and deeper understanding that we are all made as men and women in God's image for relationships of love with people of our own sex and the opposite sex. Love in its various forms is expressed in our commitments to each other and demonstrated in different ways through our bodies by means of our speech, touch and actions of service. Some physical expressions of love are fitting for some relationships and forms of commitment but not for others and some actions, even if intended to express and nurture love, do not do so.

In seeking to discern the meaning and proper forms and expressions of love, we cannot be securely guided by our own desires. This is because

---

36 The summary of biblical teaching which follows in 2.1 and 2.2 draws, with permission, heavily on the text of *FHH*, pp. 13-20 and Hilborn 2003.

our desires, like all aspects of our humanity, are fallen and disordered. Following them can thus lead to actions which are sinful and which we need to confess and turn away from in repentance. Our emotions and desires are thus not a reliable guide to God's will for our lives.[37] If we are to recognise and to delight in those patterns of life in which we will find ourselves flourishing as God intends then we need instead to look to the revealed will of the God who is love – "God's love defines our love, not the other way round."[38]

Among those patterns of love, four forms of relationship are particularly highlighted in Scripture.

First, we are born into a network of given relationships that God intends should give us love and teach us how to love from the very beginning of our lives – our *families*.

Secondly, in the course of our lives we establish loving relationships with others who become our *friends*. Indeed, "the blessing of human friendship... is sanctified by Christ who calls us his friends (John 15.13-15; cf. Is. 41.8) and elevated in him to become the 'fellowship of the Holy Spirit' (2 Cor. 13.14)".[39]

With so much current debate centering on sexual activity, it is important to reiterate the key place in God's purposes of other forms of non-erotic love such as sisterly and brotherly love *(philadelphia)*, and love expressed in friendship *(philia)*. A classic biblical example which illustrates this is that of David and Jonathan (e.g. 1 Sam. 18-19, 2 Sam. 1). Nor should we forget that Jesus chose friends whom he regarded as family (Mark 3.33-5) and that John was distinguished as "the disciple whom Jesus loved" (John 21.20). These examples confirm that we need not be fearful of deep and

---

37 For discussion of the relationship of the doctrine of sin to understanding human sexuality see David Field's two chapters in Peterson 2004, pp. 51-119.

38 *FHH*, p. 13.

39 St. Andrew's Day Statement in Bradshaw 2003, pp. 5-11 (here at pp. 9-10).

intimate same-sex friendships and should reject insinuations that such friendships must be sexual in nature.

Thirdly, the love given and received in both of these ways of life points to and is in turn deepened through our most defining loving relationship - *fellowship* with Christ and with fellow Christians in his body. He is not ashamed to call us his brothers and sisters (Heb. 2.11, 12) as well as his friends (John 15.13-15) and we are called to keep on loving one another as brothers and sisters (Heb. 13.1).

Finally, Scripture – from its account of creation in the opening chapters of Genesis (Gen. 2.18-25) through to the use of marital imagery for the eschatological consummation in Revelation (Rev. 19:7, 21:2, 9) – teaches the significance of *marriage* between a man and a woman as a distinct form of loving relationship to which many are called.

2.1.2 The importance of marriage as God's intention for sexual relationships

In Scripture and Christian tradition, the primary focus with regard to sexual relationships is not homosexuality or a person's sexuality but rather the institution of marriage. This is a loving relationship between one man and one woman that is exclusive and intended to be life-long. It is not a political creation or social construction but a good gift of God given in creation and a form of human covenant that acts as a sign of God's covenant love and faithfulness. Marriage is the only legitimate context for the total self-giving love which is expressed in sexual union. Individuals and society both flourish when the procreation and nurture of children occurs within marriage.

The early chapters of Genesis are appealed to by both Jesus and Paul. Gen 1.27-8 and Gen 2.18-24 have especially been foundational for the classical Judaeo-Christian teaching that sexual intercourse is designed for expression solely within the life-long, marital relationship of a man and a woman. They provide the basic context for Christian understanding of human sexuality, procreation and marriage. Although they do not go into great detail about the distinctions between female and male they do emphasise that each was a separate, intentional creation, and that male and female were made distinct rather than "two of the same".[40]

God's creation of the human race extends his intra-Trinitarian love outwards and opens the way to a covenant of mutual trust and care. When God sees that it is not good for Adam to be alone, he creates an 'other' – a woman – to be his companion (Gen. 2.20-5). The complementarity inherent in the resultant relationship is expressed at least partly as a physical complementarity: the two who are clearly distinct and different are nevertheless intended to become "one flesh" (Gen. 2.24). Traditional Jewish and Christian interpretation has accorded this complementarity a unique and exclusive moral status as an aspect of God's good created order, often understood in terms of natural law. It has been taken to mean that man and woman are created anatomically for each other and that, since they correspond genitally and procreatively in a way that two men or two women cannot, homosexual activity lies, by its very nature, outside the realm of divine sanction.

This view of the creation narrative has been dismissed as a 'naturalistic fallacy', leaping from 'what is' to 'what ought to be' and drawing a flawed inference of exclusive divine intentions from particular biological consequences.[41] Clearly, heterosexual sex is *itself* hardly confined to penile-vaginal penetration and reproduction but the biblical narrative

---

40 For discussions of this see Gagnon 2001; Grenz 1998; Schmidt 1995, especially pp. 39-63. The best theological study of the importance of being made male and female and its relationship to marriage is now Roberts 2007.

41 For a summary of this critique see Vasey 1995. Rowan Williams has even called this inference 'nonscriptural', apparently on the basis that while Genesis 2 may *describe* a relational norm, it should not be read as *proscribing* all exceptions to that norm (Williams 2002, p. 320). For an evangelical engagement with Williams' writing in this area see Hilborn 2002.

on men, women and sex does not suggest that the link between heterosexual activity and procreation is merely incidental. In fact, Scripture takes the procreative *capacity* of heterosexual interaction *per se* to be a distinguishing mark of its explicit divine endorsement and something which validates it over against other, intrinsically non-reproductive, forms of sexual relating (e.g. Gen. 1.28; 9.1-15; 15.1-21; Ps. 127.3).[42]

The complementarity of woman and man is much more than simply physical. Genesis 1.27 emphasises that God created human beings in His own image – male and female together – and this divine image is expressed in a relationship which may be sexual, but which is also spiritual, emotional and psychological. Being joined together in marriage becomes a fundamental expression of all this – "So a man will leave his father and his mother and be united with his wife" (Gen 2.24) – and provides the definitive biblical paradigm for human sexual love. Although this paradigm was not immediately confined to *monogamous* heterosexual marriage in the Old Testament, there can be little dispute that in biblical-theological terms heterosexual monogamy emerges from it teleologically, as its purposed end. The Genesis creation narrative is thus later taken as the basis for monogamous heterosexual marriage by both Jesus and Paul (Matt.19.4-6; Eph. 5.31). It also serves as the ground of various laws and obligations designed to reinforce the singular validity and social status of such monogamy (Matt. 19.4-12; 1 Cor. 7.1-40; Col. 3.18-19; Tit. 2.4-5; 1 Pet. 3.1-7; Heb.13.4).

Most significantly, marriage between a man and a woman is viewed in the biblical witness as a human covenant and form of union signifying God's covenant relationship with his people. This is a regular theme in the Old Testament prophets (e.g. Hosea; Jer.2.20; 3.1,20; 31.3ff; Ezek. 16 & 23; Is. 50.1; 54.6-8; 62.4ff) and is given a Christo-centric and ecclesio-centric focus by Paul in Ephesians 5. Marriage is thus to mirror God's

---

42 Further on this see Hilborn 1994.

dealings with us in terms of commitment and a promise of faithful love and provision whilst other forms of sexual relationship are forbidden in Scripture as fornication (non-marital) or adultery (extra-marital).

2.1.3 Chastity and singleness

The language of 'chastity' and a 'chaste life' is now relatively rarely used and perhaps even more rarely understood but it is central in historic Judaeo-Christian thinking about sex and has thus helped shape Western society.[43] It is often treated as simply equivalent to 'sexual abstinence when unmarried' or even 'celibate' and, in the words of an account of a Christian sexual ethic focussed on chastity, today "the word often evokes connotations of inhibition, prudery, dysfunction, and perhaps even neurosis".[44] Chastity refers, however, to a virtue which all of us – whether single or married – need to cultivate. It is a quality of mind and a power that enables us to act as we should, particularly in relation to sex. Chastity moderates and orders our desires and passions so that we act well, in a manner which serves our good and the good of others. In the words of a celebration and defence of chastity, again illustrating its counter-cultural character, "there is more to chastity than just sexual abstinence. It is the opposite of the old credit card slogan: 'Access takes the waiting out of wanting.' The 'grab it now' culture is a direct attack on chastity. Chastity properly understood is an attitude that anticipates grace; that accepts that there is a time and a place for all things."[45]

Chastity

---

43 For a study of the importance of the Judaeo-Christian concept of chastity in Western society see Riley 2000. A analysis of the economic costs of rejecting chastity and embracing 'sexual freedom' is offered in Brandon 2011, online at http://www.jubilee-centre.org/document.php?id=424.

44 Grabowski 2003, p. 71.

45 Taylor 2008, p. 4. For other realistic engagements with the challenges faced today in relation to chastity see Winner 2005 and Selmys 2009, especially pp. 147ff. (Chastity "is not a set of negative rules: 'Thou shalt not...' ...Chastity is positive: 'Thou shalt be in possession of thine own sexuality' ...The practice of chastity demonstrates that one actually possesses what one promises to give" (p. 147)). Also Simon 2012.

In this context, it is clear that living faithfully within marriage is one pattern of life within which we can nurture and display this virtue of chastity. However, many people, for Christian or other reasons, are committed to living a life of chastity when unmarried and to do so by abstaining from genital sex outside marriage. Whatever their sexuality, and whether single, divorced or widowed, they believe it right and good for them to refrain from sexual relations, however much they may long for them or for the physical bond of marriage (cf. 1 Cor. 7.11; 1 Tim. 5.9). Some of these have embraced the call to celibacy in the sense of a lifelong, rather than a provisional, commitment to the single life and sexual abstinence.

Not only did Jesus himself live chastely in the form of a single, abstinent life, he recognised and commended others who observed this pattern, as did Paul. Jesus made a distinction between those (probably impotent), who had been "born" to observe it, those (probably castrated courtiers, but possibly others) who had been "made that way by people", and those called to renounce marriage "because of the kingdom of heaven" (Matt. 19.12; cf. 1 Cor. 7.7). These points and the positive vision of the single life found in Scripture, viewing it not in terms of "an absence of" but "a freedom to and for" should not be lost as we approach those biblical texts which deal more directly with homosexual activity.[46]

2.1.4 Conclusion

Even without the specific biblical texts relating to homosexuality, this overall framework signals that according to Scripture intimate loving same-sex relationships are to be familial or forms of friendship or expressions of fellowship in Christ and as such they should not be sexual relationships. As we shall see in the next section, this is confirmed by a number of specific verses in both Old and New Testaments.

---

46 For material on singleness in the church and Christian discipleship see Danylak 2007, 2010; Deshpande 2001; Taylor 2008; Wilson 2006.

2.2 The Bible and same-sex behaviour[47]

Although "it must be acknowledged that direct references to homosexuality in Scripture are relatively few"[48] all of them – and they appear in both Old and New Testaments and a variety of biblical genres – consistently teach that homoerotic sexual practice is incompatible with God's will and thus not consistent with faithful Christian discipleship. While a number of biblical passages bear on the debate about homosexual practice, it is those from the Pauline epistles which offer the clearest and most directly relevant guidance to us as we struggle to address this issue in the present-day Church.

2.2.1 Genesis 19.1-29

The story of Lot and Sodom clearly entails a gross breach of hospitality. According to justice and tradition, the men of Sodom should have protected Lot's visitors (cf. Ezek.16.49) but they abused them. As the text suggests through its report that God aims to destroy the city (Gen. 19.12-14), and as Jesus later confirms when he denounces Sodom in Matt. 10.14-15 and 11.20-4, the men's actions are a manifestation of much deeper-seated sins of idolatry, pride and rebellion. These sins are strong themes of the passage but this cannot mask the fact that the abuse in question does appear to have strongly sexual connotations.

Some of the early scholars attempting to reinterpret biblical texts in this area, notably Derrick Bailey and John Boswell, denied this sexual element. They claimed that in verse 5 the verb usually translated 'know' means simply 'get acquainted with' rather than 'have sex with'. Although the verb

---

47 What follows is a brief summary of why these texts are understood to lead to the rejection of all homosexual activity. For those wishing to explore different readings, the "traditional" interpretation is helpfully presented alongside and in dialogue with an alternative, "revisionist" reading of the same texts in both Via and Gagnon 2003 and Grimsrud and Nation 2008.

48 *FHH*, p. 12.

is used in a sexual sense on just 15 other occasions out of 943 uses in the Hebrew Bible, the context here is one in which Lot himself seems to have viewed the intentions of the men of Sodom as sexual. In addition, there are clear semantic and narrative parallels between this account and that of the rape of the Levite's concubine in Jdg. 19.22, 25 (which quite explicitly uses the verb 'know' in a sexual way). This explains why Nissinen, who rejects some traditional interpretations of the classic texts, is clear that "the sexual aspect of the actions of the men of Sodom cannot be gainsaid"[49] and Gagnon concludes that "few scholars today, even among supporters of homoerotic behavior, adopt Bailey's argument."[50]

From a Christian point of view, it is also relevant that, in the New Testament, both Peter (2 Pet. 2.10) and Jude (verse 7) seem to regard Sodom's sin as at least partly to do with disordered sexual behaviour. Peter writes of those who, like the men in Genesis 19, "indulge their flesh in depraved lust" and Jude describes the same "sexual immorality" and "unnatural lust" as an example of sin prone to merit the "punishment of eternal fire". As Robert Gagnon points out in his exhaustive study of this and other relevant texts on sexual immorality, it is noteworthy that Peter and Jude highlight the sin of lust here, rather than any failure to provide social justice or hospitality.

Nevertheless, the intended sexual act is one of gang rape. This, as in the parallel incident in Judges 19, renders this passage less relevant to the present day theological issue (of non-violent, consenting homosexual practice) although Davidson states "that the opprobrium attached to the Sodomites' intended activity involved not only rape but the inherent degradation of same-sex intercourse is confirmed by the intertextual linkages between Ezekiel and the sexual 'abominations' mentioned in Levitical legislation".[51]

---

49 Nissinen 1998, p. 46.

50 Gagnon 2001, p. 74.

51 Davidson 2007, p. 149. The key verses in Ezekiel which point to a sexual element in Sodom's sin are Ezekiel 16.43, 50.

2.2.2 Leviticus 18.22 and 20.13

These verses could conceivably refer to cult prostitution and if so would not be directly relevant to the question of faithful, loving same-sex relationships. Nissinen, however, warns that "the conclusion that Leviticus 18.22 and 20.13 refer solely to homosexual acts related to cultic practices...leaves many things hanging in the air".[52] The orientation of both chapters is against *all* forms of ungodly sexual behaviour - incest, adultery and bestiality as well as homosexual practice. These are viewed as a threat to marriage and the family, each of which plays a pivotal role in Hebrew culture and religion. They are deemed wrong not simply because pagan Canaanites indulged in them, but because God has pronounced them wrong as such.

Attempts to limit the prohibitions' scope in other ways also fail. Lev. 18.22, in declaring "You shall not lie with a male", seems to prohibit men from taking the 'active' role in homosexual intercourse, even though this was deemed to be comparatively respectable in several contemporary cultures, as compared to the 'passive' role. The text also deploys the generic term 'male' rather than any more specific word for 'man' or 'youth'. This also points to a more comprehensive understanding of homoerotic activity. Furthermore, the death penalty in Lev. 20.13 applies equally to the active and the passive partner. There is thus no implication of rape, in which case the rapist alone would have been executed (cf. Deut. 22.22-5), or any hint of coercion. The context would thus seem to include homosexual intercourse by mutual consent. Comparative literary study has revealed that the Assyrians outlawed forcible same-sex intercourse and that the Egyptians banned pederasty (older men having sexual relations with younger boys). Israel appears to have stood alone in viewing homosexual acts in general with this degree of severity.[53]

---

52 Nissinen 1998, p. 41.

53 For further discussion of this text, particularly in its original context, see Wold 1998, Gagnon 2001, pp. 111-46 and Davidson 2007, pp. 149-59.

The question, however, remains as to whether Old Testament teaching on this matter is superseded by the new covenant in Christ, who makes all things clean and teaches the centrality of love. Among evangelicals there are a number of different approaches to working out the contemporary relevance of Mosaic law. It is clear that Jesus mitigated the law's prescribed punishments but that in so doing he did not deny that the actions condemned by the law were wrong. This is seen most powerfully in relation to the penalty of stoning for adultery (which applied equally to homoerotic sexual practice). This is effectively challenged by Jesus in John 8.1-11. Nonetheless, he upholds the moral prohibition behind the penalty when he tells the woman caught in adultery: "sin no more".

Through the centuries, many Christians have drawn on this and other New Testament teaching to distinguish different types of Old Testament law. The civil law and its penalties were related and limited to ancient Israelite society while the ceremonial laws were fulfilled by Christ, particularly by his sacrificial death on the cross. The moral law is, however, upheld by Christ and so in force for the church. Whatever one's view of this civil-ceremonial-moral distinction within Old Testament laws (and imposing this construct and attempting to draw such distinctions is questioned by many), the continuing relevance of these laws is confirmed in the New Testament, especially by the apostolic reaffirmation of them in Pauline texts dealing with homosexuality.

2.2.3 The Gospels

Apologists for lesbian and gay sexual relationships point out that Jesus himself does not pronounce explicitly on homosexual practice but arguments from silence are notoriously suspect. Jesus hardly commented in direct terms on every ethical issue under the sun. The gospels give us no explicit teaching from him on slavery or even on idolatry. Furthermore, not only did he affirm marriage between a man and a woman based on Genesis, his condemnations of *porneia* or sexual immorality in Matt. 15.19 and Mark 7.21 would almost definitely have been meant, and been understood, to include homoerotic sexual activity. As Michael Satlow has shown, such activity was typically condemned by the rabbis of the time whenever they considered it.[54] We can therefore be confident that, in the words of gospels' scholar John Nolland, "in the Jewish context of Jesus' day, and in the Christian context that grew out of it, homosexual coitus would have been automatically embraced within the scope of *porneia*".[55]

2.2.4 Romans 1.18-32

Romans 1 is without doubt the most important biblical reference for the homosexuality debate as it provides by far the fullest *theological* reflection on same-sex sexual relations in the biblical canon and is almost certainly the only reference in Scripture to lesbian sexual activity.[56] As already noted in chapter one the context underlines the equal status of all Christians with respect to salvation (v.16), while at the same time showing our equality with respect to divine "wrath" (v.18) and "judgement" (2.3).

Idolatrous exchanges and disordered sexual behaviour

Paul describes a "godlessness" (*asebeian*, v 18) which is demonstrated in both the *apathetic neglect* of God that fails to honour his purpose as revealed in the world and the more active idolatry which provides the key to interpretation of verses 26 and 27. In verse 23, Paul presents the first of three vital "exchanges". He states here that the wicked characteristically "changed (*ēllaxan*) the glory of the immortal God into images resembling

---

54 Satlow 1995.

55 Nolland 2009, p. 25. See also Gagnon 2001, pp. 185-228.

56 For the fullest discussion of female homosexuality in the New Testament and early Christianity see Brooten 1996.

a mortal human being or birds or four-footed animals or reptiles". This is broadened as "they exchanged (*ēllaxan*) the truth about God for a lie and worshipped and served the creature rather than the Creator" (v.25, cf. Ex. 20.1-3). The idolatrous exchange of creature and Creator in v.25 is literally *the* lie (*tō pseudei*) - the defining distortion of God's purpose for the world. From this defining distortion other distortions inevitably follow (cf. Gen. 3.5). So Paul casts homosexual practice against the backdrop not only of Mosaic law, but also of natural law, in relation to Genesis 1-3: humankind made "male and female" in God's image and their complementarity as "one flesh" (Gen. 1.27; 2.24).

It is as archetypes of such distortions that we must approach the degrading and shameful uses of the body *(atimadzesthai ta sōmata).* These are described generically in v.24 and illustrated specifically in relation to same-sex intercourse in vv.26-7. Although these belong to a much broader catalogue of evils (cf. v.29ff), within the structure of Paul's argument such bodily degradations are marked out for special attention because they constitute a particularly vivid paradigm of creation gone wrong. Although we may assume from v.24 that Paul is thinking of heterosexual as well as homosexual depravities, the third "exchange" in vv.26-7 suggests Paul sees homoerotic activity as almost iconic of what he is condemning. Richard B. Hays thus writes of engaging in homosexual behavior as enacting "an outward and visible sign of an inward and spiritual reality: the rejection of the Creator's design".[57]

A creation-theological reading of verses 26-7 thus derives from the *broad contours* of Paul's discourse, and not a dogmatic eisegesis of the single words "nature" and "natural" (*phusin, phusikēn*) in vv.26-7. Despite carrying other meanings in Scripture, sometimes culturally-specific (as in 1 Cor. 11.14), and sometimes negative (Eph. 2.3), the pervasiveness of Paul's wider argument from design here means we cannot divorce *phusin* from

---

57 Hays 1996, p. 386. For a powerful polemical defence of a traditional sexual ethic based on this understanding see Scott 2004.

the apostle's understanding of God's eternal intent for humans (cf. v.20). Furthermore, the notion of homosexual practice as against or beyond nature (*para phusin*) and thus immoral is found in several contemporary Graeco-Roman sources, especially in that Hellenistic Jewish tradition with which Paul himself was associated.[58]

God "giving people up"

There is also a somewhat surprising twist in Paul's reasoning, namely the identification of God as actively "giving people up" to the lusts of their hearts. This concept is mediated no fewer than three times by the use of the verb *parēdōken* (vv.24, 26, 28). It implies that all forms of disordered sexual desires – the lusts of our hearts – are a manifestation of sin. They have about them a deeply embedded, and even unconscious, compulsiveness. This, after a time, hardens itself even against the will of the Creator. In such circumstances, Paul envisages what Mark Bonnington and Bob Fyall describe as a "terrible divine 'hands off'", or what Hays sees as the "irony of sin [playing] itself out" – an irony in which the creature's original instinct for glorification is wrathfully loosed by the Creator into doomed self-destruction.[59]

The sexual misconduct abhorred by Paul is thus the *result* of divine judgement – on fallen human society and culture, not specific individuals – rather than the *cause* of it. It is therefore as much to be regretted as castigated: it is a presenting symptom of a world estranged from its Maker. It is a mark of that universal fallenness in which we all share, and Paul correlates it with an idolatrous culture, suggesting that the more idolatrous a culture, the more it will distort the sexual norms and model God has given us. Sexual misconduct therefore should not be singled out for particular scorn, even while it cannot be condoned.

---

58 See Gagnon 2001, pp. 254-70.

59 Bonnington and Fyall 1996, p. 20 and Hays 1996, p. 386.

Interpreting same-sex sexual behaviour theologically

In the light of this theological superstructure of Romans 1-2, closer analysis can be offered of verses 26-7 themselves. Few serious scholars doubt that when Paul here condemns the use of human bodies "against nature" (*para phusin*), he has in mind sexual acts performed by men with men, and by women with women. Although the latter has been questioned, the clear rhetorical and grammatical parallels between women and men, the latter of whom are explicitly said to have abandoned heterosexual practices (*krēsin tēs thleias*) for homosexual ones (*orexei autōn eis allēlous*) tells against alternative interpretations of certain heterosexual conduct by women. The focus is on sexual relations as such, rather than on specific sexual techniques. In addition, Paul uses the more generalised vocabulary of "male" and "female" here (*arsenes; thēleias*), rather than the terminology of "men" or "women" (*gunē; anēr*).[60]

But does Paul include *all* forms of sexual relationship between people of the same gender? Some have argued his concern is a particular form of pagan temple prostitution. Even Boswell, however, admits this explanation falters as soon as one realizes that the parties involved in the sexual activities defined by Paul are "burning with lust" for one another (v.27). This is unlikely to fit the more dispassionate prostitution associated with religious ceremony and ritual. Others hold Paul is concerned primarily with pederasty – a practice restricted to the upper echelons of society and indulged in by married men and the most common manifestation of homosexual practice in ancient Greece. There is, however, no female equivalent and this was by no means the *only* recognised form of same-sex relationship. We cannot know for certain the full range of homosexual relationships and practices with which Paul was familiar but his virtually unprecedented yoking of lesbianism with male

---

60 Brooten 1996 is the major study here. Personally she expresses a hope that "churches today...will no longer teach Romans 1.26f as authoritative" (p. 302) but, exploring in some detail those who argue against a reference to lesbianism, she is clear that "'unnatural intercourse' refers specifically to sexual relations between women" (p. 249).

homosexuality suggests his perspective is unusually broad for his time.[61] Finally, some, following Boswell, argue that Paul is only concerned with those who are 'naturally' heterosexual but engage in homosexual activity. However, as Hays has argued in detail, Paul here

> is not presenting biographical sketches of individual pagans; he is offering an apocalyptic 'long view' which indicts fallen humanity as a whole... the charge that these fallen humans have 'exchanged natural relations for unnatural' means nothing more nor less than that human beings, created for heterosexual companionship as the Genesis story bears witness, have distorted even so basic a truth as their sexual identity by rejecting the male and female roles which are 'naturally' theirs in God's created order. The charge is a corporate indictment of pagan society, not a narrative about the 'rake's progress' of particular individuals. [62]

The most authentic reading of Rom. 1.26-7 remains therefore that which sees Paul prohibiting homosexual activity in the most general of terms, rather than in respect of more culturally and historically specific forms of such activity.

2.2.5 1 Timothy 1.8-11 and 1 Corinthians 6.9

1 Tim. 1.8-11 warns us against crude law-grace dichotomies. The need to integrate legal/doctrinal rectitude ("the law is good", v.8) with "love that comes from a pure heart, conscience, and sincere faith" (v.6) is central. One of Paul's concerns here is contraventions of "sound doctrine". As part of his list of those who commit such contraventions in verses 9-10 we encounter the word *arsenokoites* which appears also in a similar Pauline list of vices at 1 Cor. 6.9-11. Most translations and commentaries associate

---

61 For evidence on ancient homosexuality and its relevance to Paul's argument see Smith 1996.

62 Hays 1986, p. 200.

arsenokoites in some way or other with practitioners of homoerotic acts. If, as G.W. Knight and others argue, the sins catalogued in 1 Tim. 1.9-10 are "a deliberate echo of the order of the second part of the Decalogue"[63] then Paul views those who undermine the seventh commandment as fornicators (*pornois*) and *arsenokoites*. Thus, both homosexual *and* heterosexual dimensions of sexual immorality are explicitly dealt with and both are seen as undermining the sanctity of marriage.

At first sight, precise interpretation of the word *arsenokoites* appears difficult as there is no record of its use in pre-Christian literature. It is, however, a compound of two terms which carried familiar sexual connotations: *arsēn* was a specific word for male, but was often used in connection with male sexuality, while *koitēs* usually meant 'bed', but functioned as a widespread euphemism for sexual intercourse (cf. our term *coitus*). Paul's yoking of the two therefore points strongly to a homoerotic denotation. In fact, *arsenokoites* seems most probably to have been coined by Paul in response to the vocabulary of the Septuagint version of Lev. 18.22 and 20.13 where its constituent terms appear as a translation of the Hebrew *mishkav zakur* ("lying with a male").

The context of Paul's remarks in both 1 Timothy 1 and 1 Corinthians 6 is eligibility for God's kingdom in general, and for church membership in particular. Homoerotic sexual practice here again belongs to a catalogue of sins, apparently no better, and no worse, than fornication, adultery, theft, greed, drunkenness, slander and robbery. In addition to disallowing the singling out of homosexual sin for special condemnation this also suggests that early church congregations contained what we would call homosexual people (cf. 1 Cor. 6.11). Although some of these may still have been sexually active, the clear teaching of Paul is that continuing attachment to this, as to the other sinful practices he mentions, is incompatible with authentic participation in the community of God's people. In this Paul is consistent with the witness of Scripture as a whole.

---

63 Knight 1992, p. 85.

2.2.6 Conclusion on biblical teaching

In conclusion, Scripture opposes any affirmation of same-sex sexual behaviour both in terms of its overall vision of human sexuality within God's works of creation and redemption and in specific biblical texts in Old and New Testaments which address the subject directly.

Sexuality in the biblical story as a whole

Scripture from Genesis to Revelation witnesses to the goodness of God's creation of humans as male and female and the union of a man and a woman in marriage. It is, however, also clear, from its account of God's response to our rejection of his will in Genesis 3 onwards, that our rejection of God brings disorder into all our relationships, affections and behaviour, including those related to sex. This means that our experience and participation in God's creational gifts of sexual otherness and sexual union are not as they should be but need to be redeemed and healed. Scripture, in the history of Israel and the teaching of Jesus and the apostles, progressively reveals to us the form of that redemption and healing in human life. This includes, as fully lived out by Jesus himself, intimate, loving non-sexual relationships for those who are not married and also faithful commitment within the sexual union of marriage, whose bond between those who are created by God as male and female is a 'one flesh' union that acts as a sign of God's covenantal relationship with humanity and the union between Christ and his church. The Scriptures authorise no other form of life as expressing God's purposes in creation and redemption and consistently warn against forms of behaviour that abandon these two paths.

The specific texts on homosexuality

Although various attempts continue to be made to re-interpret or narrow the meaning of the biblical texts referring explicitly to same-sex sexual behaviour,[64] the traditional evangelical stance remains secure. Indeed, it has been significantly strengthened by the writings of various scholars,[65] particularly the monumental work on Old Testament sexuality by Richard M. Davidson[66] and the writings of New Testament scholar Richard Hays.[67] The detailed and extensive study by New Testament scholar Robert Gagnon *(The Bible and Homosexual Practice)* remains unanswered by those who reject his conclusions.[68] The conclusion reached by the Church of England's House of Bishops in 2003 remains a reasonable summary of the situation:

> *The various suggestions for revising the traditional view of the biblical material have not succeeded in changing the consensus of scholarly opinion about the meaning of the key passages in Leviticus and the New Testament. At the moment, the traditional understanding of these passages remains the most convincing one in the minds of most biblical scholars.[69]*

---

64 It is important that evangelicals understand the arguments of those who defend homosexuality not by dismissing or overturning Scripture but by claiming Scripture as the basis for seeking to revise traditional teaching. Rogers 2009 is a good guide to such a perspective.

65 See, for example, Seitz 2000, Goddard and Walker 2003, Humphrey 2003, Peterson's three chapters in Peterson 2004 and Goldingay 2010.

66 Davidson 2007.

67 Hays 1996, chapter 16 which appears in a shorter form in Dunnam and Malony 2003 (pp. 65-84), a significant collection of essays from American Methodists.

68 Gagnon 2001. Gagnon also regularly responds to critics and their attempts to reinterpret Scripture with articles published on his website at www.robgagnon.net

69 Church of England House of Bishops 2003, 4.4.34.

Comparison with other areas of disagreement or development

The consistent negative witness of both Testaments is a crucial feature that distinguishes this subject from others such as slavery, the role of women or remarriage after divorce. Homosexuality is sometimes erroneously compared with these in order to argue that a more affirming stance in relation to same-sex behaviour is consonant with an evangelical view of Scripture. In these areas it is possible to discern a trajectory within Scripture's progressive revelation set in its cultural contexts and to interpret more restrictive texts in the context of both more permissive ones and a wider biblical theology (in relation to slavery, gender or marriage). This gives a scriptural basis for development in Christian teaching and practice which is not possible in relation to homosexuality. There, in various cultural contexts, all of them more affirming of same-sex sexual behaviour, the biblical writers always univocally reject such conduct among God's people:[70]

> *Whilst the church now approaches slavery, contraception, divorce and remarriage, and the role of women in leadership in ways that differ from historical practices, nevertheless, the church has not in these areas rejected Scripture but learned to understand it better. In the case of homosexuality, the church has not understood its reading of the Bible to require development because here, unlike the other examples, there is a consistent negative witness throughout the Bible. A major danger today is that claims of being led by the Spirit to change the teaching of the Bible can very easily disguise attempts to accommodate the Christian gospel to the spirit of the age. There is no authority given to human beings to change the plain truth of Scripture.[71]*

---

70 A helpful discussion of the differences and development of a hermeneutical method is Webb 2001 who discusses the issues specifically in relation to women and homosexuality more briefly at Webb 2004 (on which see also France 2000). The Mennonite scholar Willard Swartley who explored issues relating to hermeneutics and a number of contentious subjects in *Slavery, Sabbath, War and Women* (Swartley 1983) has explained and defended his stance in relation to homosexuality in Swartley 2003.

71 Don Horrocks in Chalke and Mann 2010, p. 123.

The acceptance of homosexual conduct by the Church is therefore not a legitimate theological development as it would overturn the consistent testimony of Scripture. Scripture must be the test for any claims of Spirit-led innovation, and where there are tensions with our context Scripture should offer a critique of changing social and ethical norms rather than being abandoned in the face of such cultural change.

Consequences of Scripture's teaching

This understanding of Scripture's sexual ethic has a number of consequences for Christian teaching and pastoral practice:

1. Our primary concern regarding sexual relationships should, as explained above, be the positive one of upholding marriage as, in the words of the affirmation, "the only form of partnership approved by God for sexual relations". Any discussion of same-sex relationships can only take its proper place and make sense in the light of this vision. Emphasising and living out this understanding is increasingly counter-cultural given the rise in sexual experimentation and promiscuity, 'hook-ups' and heterosexual cohabitation as well as the increased acceptance of homosexual behaviour. [72]

2. Homosexual behaviour is sinful, but it should not be subject to greater censure or disapproval than heterosexual fornication or adultery or non-sexual sins such as pride or gluttony. Care needs to be taken to avoid a double standard where concern about possible sexual immorality in non-marital relationships focuses on same-sex relationships.

3. Scripture's concern is with homosexual *behaviour*. It does not address the categories of experience we have described in terms of same-sex

---

72 For insightful analyses of our changing sexual culture and Christian responses to it see Brandon 2009, Kuehne 2009 and Simon 2012. The influence of 'queer theory' in reshaping contemporary society's understandings of gender and sexuality is explored and critiqued in Sanlon 2010.

attraction and *orientation* or the concept of sexual *identity*. Scripture does offer us positive models of loving, intimate but non-sexual same-sex *relationships* (most famously David and Jonathan but also Ruth and Naomi, Jesus and his disciples, Paul and Timothy).

4. Especially for the growing proportion of the population which is unmarried, the church needs to be a place where single people are valued and non-sexual relationships of love and intimacy are nurtured within the fellowship of believers and through the families and friendships which are part of it. Hays rightly states that "within the Church we need to shatter the power of the myth that…only marriage offers the conditions necessary for human fulfilment. We must work with compassion at recovering a vision for singleness as an authentic vocation." [73]

2.3 Christian tradition

For evangelicals, Scripture is the supreme authority, but Christian tradition is an important subordinate authority and a guide when evaluating competing interpretations of Scripture.[74] Although unable to be explored in detail here, it is, therefore, also important to note that the reading of Scripture outlined above is one shared by the overwhelming majority of Christians (and, in relation to the Old Testament, Jews) down through the centuries and supported by most academic theologians and biblical scholars.

As noted in the discussion of "the witness of history" found in *FHH*, "the Church has consistently regarded same-sex sexual activity as wrong" although "mainstream Christianity has rarely stigmatised it as the worst of sins".[75] As a result, "evangelical Christians should be in no doubt: the endorsement of homosexual relationships as on a par with heterosexual

---

73 Hays 1996, p. 373.

74 For a helpful guide on evangelicals and tradition see Holmes 2002.

75 *FHH*, p. 25.

relationships expressed in marriage would represent a serious departure from the teaching of the Church throughout the ages, as well as from the teaching of Scripture".[76]

2.4 Gay and lesbian people and homophobia

Evangelicals and gay and lesbian people

One of the most remarked-upon and welcomed features of *FHH* was its confession of evangelical participation in a wider failing of church and society:

> *We acknowledge with sadness that within the evangelical community, as in the wider church and society as a whole, there is still a significant degree of fear, misunderstanding, prejudice and even openly expressed hostility towards homosexual people. Where homophobia means 'irrational hatred or hostility' towards such people, we condemn it in the strongest possible terms and see it as a cause for repentance.*[77]

This then found expression in two of *FHH*'s affirmations which have shaped the affirmation at the start of this chapter that:

> *We affirm God's love and concern for all human beings, whatever their sexuality, and so repudiate all attitudes and actions which victimise or diminish people whose affections are directed towards people of the same sex. We are encouraged many Christians now recognise and deeply regret the hurt caused by past and present failures in their responses to those who experience same-sex attraction.*

Sadly, at the time of *FHH*, such statements were viewed as surprising but they did reflect a growing awareness among evangelicals of our serious

---

76 *FHH*, p. 27.

77 *FHH*, p. 6.

failure in these areas. Already, in 1995, Thomas Schmidt, while defending biblical teaching, had acknowledged that "Our heterosexual sin includes sins of hatred toward homosexuals". He illustrated this with reference to what he called "attitudinal" discrimination and victimization expressed in using or tolerating "slang terms, demeaning jokes or derogatory offhand comments".[78] Anglican John Stott admitted that "love is just what the church has generally failed to show to homosexual people".[79] Baptist Stanley Grenz described homophobia – "hatred or devaluing of persons for no other reasons than because they are sexually aroused by persons of the same sex" – as a prejudice akin to racism or anti-Semitism, which Christians ought to combat and needed to recognise was "prevalent in the church".[80]

Although the Evangelical Alliance's statements in *FHH* and subsequently, together with wider social awareness of this evil, have impacted on evangelical thought and practice it remains an area where further work is needed both theologically and practically. Relatively little has been done to articulate why Christians need to repent in this area or what specifically is being repudiated and regretted.[81]

Homophobia and the challenge of defining terms

Part of the problem faced in relation to challenging wrong attitudes and behaviour is that of terminology and definitions. This is why the affirmation summarising biblical theology and an evangelical sexual ethic also states that we do not accept that holding these views on biblical grounds "is in itself homophobic". The common understanding of homophobia has been shaped by a rights-based philosophy and political campaigns for the full acceptance of homosexuality and

---

78 Schmidt 1995, p. 172.

79 Stott 1998, pp. 45-6.

80 Grenz 1998, pp. 149-50.

81 One resource, drawn on for the discussion here, is Goddard 2006b.

against traditional Christian teaching. As a result, disagreeing with such campaigns and articulating traditional Christian teaching has come to be falsely labelled as homophobic. It is important that those who take such stances and raise reasoned arguments in public debate against society normalising homosexual behaviour are not subjected to insult and dismissal of their views by such a misuse of terms. This is unfair on those who hold seriously considered convictions concerning sexual ethics. It also prevents the proper naming of unacceptable attitudes and behaviours towards gay and lesbian people that need to be identified and challenged.

Attempts to redefine homophobia in terms of "an irrational fear or hatred of homosexuals" are, however, problematic. They can give the impression that there is a rational fear or hatred of homosexuals which is not being repudiated. A Christian stance is based rather on what our affirmation describes as "God's love and concern for all human beings, whatever their sexuality". This stems from what the Evangelical Alliance basis of faith confesses as our belief in "the dignity of all people, made male and female in God's image".

In this light, perhaps the most helpful articulation of a Christian stance fully consistent with the sexual ethic outlined above is that found in a statement in 2005 from Anglican leaders across the world:

> In our discussion and assessment of the moral appropriateness of specific human behaviours, we continue unreservedly to be committed to the pastoral support and care of homosexual people. The victimisation or diminishment of human beings whose affections happen to be ordered towards people of the same sex is anathema to us.[82]

82 Communiqué by the Primates of the Anglican Communion meeting at Dromantine, 24th February 2005 (para 6). Such a stance can enable those who hold different views on sexual ethics to stand together against such behaviour as evidenced by www.dontthrowstones.info.

Most obviously this requires Christian condemnation of all violence against people because of their sexuality.[83] It must, however, extend further to include rejecting and opposing all demeaning, bullying, marginalising or scaremongering attitudes and speech. We must also challenge all forms of discrimination towards someone on the grounds of their sexual attractions, orientation or identity. If we are repudiating and expressing regret then this also needs to be expressed positively. This means nurturing and modelling patterns of behaviour – personally and corporately – that assure gay and lesbian people both inside and outside the church that they are "loved and valued by God" and "deserving of the best we can give of pastoral care and friendship".[84] What that means in pastoral practice is the concern of the next three chapters.

2.5 Conclusion

In developing a gospel-based response to issues relating to homosexuality, the Evangelical Alliance makes the two affirmations which head this chapter as truths which evangelicals need to live by. In practice it can at times feel as if there is a tension between them and, as so often in Christian history and today, difficulties arise when one truth is affirmed but another is ignored or even denied.

One challenge these twin truths present for evangelicals is in their teaching and preaching ministries. Some will be tempted not to teach God's revealed will for sexual relationships clearly from Scripture because of its increasingly counter-cultural character or fear of being considered homophobic. In such situations there needs to be a renewed confidence

---

83 This is, sadly, still a reality even in Britain today as evidenced by the conviction in January 2011 of two young people for the murder of Ian Baynham in Trafalgar Square after subjecting him to homophobic insults.

84 Communique by the Primates of the Anglican Communion meeting at Dromantine, 24th February 2005 (para 6).

in the truth and power of biblical teaching and a setting of the specific question of homosexuality within the wider vision of human sexuality – created, broken and restored – which Scripture provides. At the other pole, some Christians may be so concerned to defend biblical teaching that they over-emphasise this area and do not always clearly also uphold the truth of God's universal love and concern or challenge homophobic attitudes and actions.

It is vital that teaching in this area, while giving due weight to the pressing issues and challenges raised by our cultural context, is proportionate to its biblical significance. Whenever someone is speaking and teaching on the subject of homosexuality it is important they do so with a pastoral rather than a political focus. This means, for example, that it is wise to assume that there is at least one person listening who experiences same-sex attraction. In both content and tone what is said must therefore both make clear what Scripture teaches but also make it easier, not harder, for hearers to be assured of God's grace and to feel the church is a safe place to share their situation and struggles with fellow Christians.

Only when there is a clear commitment from evangelicals to teach and live by both of these affirmations can a gospel-based community of grace be established which offers Christ-like pastoral care.

Chapter Three

Developing a Framework for Pastoral Reflection and Practice

Affirmations

(4) We encourage evangelical congregations to be communities of grace in which those who experience same-sex attraction and seek to live faithfully in accordance with biblical teaching are welcomed and affirmed. Such Christians need churches which are safe spaces where they are able to share and explore their stories with fellow believers for mutual encouragement and support as we help each other grow together into maturity in Christ.

(5) We oppose moves within certain churches to accept and/or endorse sexually active same-sex partnerships as a legitimate form of Christian relationship and to permit the ordination to ministry of those in such sexual relationships. We stand prayerfully with those in such churches who are seeking to resist these moves on biblical grounds.

(6) We oppose church services of blessing for civil partnerships and other forms of gay and lesbian relationships as unbiblical and reject any redefinition of marriage to encompass same-sex relationships.

(7) We commend and encourage all those who experience same-sex attraction and have committed themselves to chastity by refraining from homoerotic sexual practice. We believe they should be eligible for ordination and leadership within the church, recognising that they can bring invaluable insights and experience to the sphere of Christian pastoral ministry.

In the light of the three affirmations made in the opening two chapters, this chapter begins to consider their practical outworking in the life of the Christian community and in particular our pastoral response in the area of homosexuality. It is wise to avoid being too specific here given the uniqueness of each situation. Nevertheless, based on the biblical teaching about marriage and human sexuality summarised in chapter two and the rejection of homophobic attitudes, the Evangelical Alliance makes the four affirmations above. This chapter sets these affirmations in the context of a framework and some basic general principles for pastoral reflection and practice. This framework and principles can then also guide responses in more specific scenarios such as those explored in chapters four and five.

The principles behind these four affirmations and shaping the next two chapters focus on two different areas. First, there is a further exploration of the crucial distinction between orientation and practice. This was introduced, along with the five sub-categories within these two areas, in chapter one. Secondly, there is the question of the proper relationship between the private and the public realms.

3.1 Distinguishing orientation and practice

In the analysis of chapter one it was suggested (in 1.5) that the common general distinction between orientation and practice contained a number of further distinctions within it and that there were, in fact, five areas of human experience and conduct that were included under 'homosexuality'. These now require some further explanation.

3.1.1 Attraction, orientation and identity

Using the work of Yarhouse it was argued that language of 'orientation' needed to distinguish three different aspects:

- the experience of *same-sex attraction*
- the recognition - given the pattern of those attractions - that one has a *same-sex orientation*
- the embracing of a *gay identity*.

Attraction and orientation

In relation to sexual *attraction* and *orientation* the fundamental reality here is that these are primarily experiences of desire which someone has and discoveries they make about themselves rather than consciously made choices or actions of the will. Some of our attractions may be shaped in various ways by our choices and acts of will. Usually, however, they are much more 'givens' or constraints for which we are not responsible or blameworthy. They are, in other words, aspects of our lived experience, affections and personality within which we are called to discern and live out what it means to be a faithful disciple of Christ.

In pastoral situations where this is the focus, the first two affirmations made above (in chapters one and two) will be the guiding principles. The St. Andrew's Day Statement provides wise counsel as it sets these aspects of our sexuality in the broader context of our common fallen humanity and the hope we share in Christ. Recalling its earlier statement that we are "adopted as children of God and called to follow in the way of the cross", the authors write:

> *We all are summoned to various forms of self-denial. The struggle against disordered desires, or the misdirection of innocent desires, is part of every Christian's life, consciously undertaken in baptism. In any individual case, the form which this struggle takes may be determined by circumstances (wealth or poverty, illness or health, educational success or failure). Often these are not open to choice, but are given to us as a situation in which we are to live faithfully. We are not promised that the struggle will be quickly and triumphantly resolved, nor even that it will be successful at every point along*

the way; only that it will be crowned at last by a character formed through patience to be like Christ's.[85]

A central pastoral calling here is therefore to discern in relation to our experience of sexual attraction and orientation what are "disordered desires", what would be "the misdirection of innocent desires", and how we struggle against these and help each other in our struggles. In relation to same-sex attraction, this is something where, although we all have a contribution to make, it is particularly important to hear the wisdom of those Christians who experience such attractions and who struggle in their own lives to direct them aright and to resist those they judge to be disordered.

Sexual identity

In relation to *identity*, there is more of a conscious self-identification. This may – but need not – involve an expression of social and political solidarity with others who share that identity and thus go beyond simply recognition of personal *attraction* or *orientation*. In cases of such solidarity, gay identity can be linked to a strong rejection of biblical teaching and this is often the case in the secular world. Sometimes it can – either explicitly or implicitly – even become a form of spirituality in which a person gains their sense of worth, belonging and self-understanding at a deep level from their sexual identity. This explains why there can be a strong reaction when that identity is questioned or critiqued and why references to "loving the sinner but hating the sin" are often rejected.

It is, however, important to recognise that none of these other aspects found within a gay identity follow automatically simply from someone identifying as "gay'" or "lesbian". That is a decision about how to describe

---

85 Bradshaw 2003, pp. 7-8.

oneself based on one's experience of sexual attraction/orientation. For some it may be no more than a way of being at peace with who they feel themselves to be instead of fighting against it internally. In such situations it is an identity which carries no necessary consequences in terms of their wider conduct sexually or politically. A gay or lesbian identity can thus be fully compatible with living out the third affirmation concerning a Christian sexual ethic as a single, celibate lesbian or gay man.

There are a number of important questions raised for Christians in relation to how such an identity relates to other aspects of who one is – particularly one's fundamental and central identity in Christ – and how embracing such an identity is understood in wider church and society. Nevertheless, 'identity' is best understood as a distinctive aspect of 'orientation' rather than 'practice' as it involves identifying and naming one's attraction or orientation. These issues will be discussed further in chapter four (especially at 4.2.4).

3.1.2 Practice – behaviour and relationships

It was argued in chapter one that, in thinking about what is usually called 'homosexual practice', there were two key areas that needed to be considered – homosexual *behaviour* (or "homoerotic sexual practice") and same-sex *relationships*. Here there are clear conscious decisions being made to act in certain ways. Such actions usually affect other people and those acting are, to some degree, morally responsible for these actions, certainly to a much greater degree than they are in relation to their attraction or orientation. This means patterns of behaviour and relationship cannot be treated in the same way as issues focussed on 'orientation'.

The practical implications drawn from the orientation/practice distinction in the affirmations above and in chapters four and five obviously reflect the evangelical stance of the third affirmation. It is, however, important to realise that the distinction itself is one which everyone makes to some degree. The experience of certain attractions (even when they amount to an orientation) or the assumption of a particular sexual (for example, LGB) identity does not tell a person how to behave or relate sexually. It does not determine what sexual behaviour or relationships are acceptable. It does not entail acceptance of all patterns of acting on those attractions or living out that identity. Whether and how to act on those attractions or live out that identity is therefore a further matter involving moral discernment. A person's sexual attractions, orientation or identity does not absolve them of moral accountability before God and other people for their practice in terms of their sexual behaviour and relationships.

In relation to sexual practice, the first and second affirmations must continue to shape any Christian response. In addition, the third affirmation now also comes to bear on pastoral practice. In relation to *behaviour* there is the need to consider the consequences of biblical teaching that homoerotic sexual practice is incompatible with God's will as revealed in Scripture. In relation to *relationships* there will be a concern that no other relationship is treated as equivalent to marriage and that the principle is unambiguously upheld that monogamous heterosexual marriage is the only form of partnership approved by God for sexual relations. The pastoral outworkings of this are explored more fully in chapter five.

3.2 Relating public and private

In seeking to create a community of grace it is important – particularly in relation to issues of sexuality – to recognise and uphold distinctions between the private and public spheres. Part of the challenge here is that there are degrees of privacy and publicity. The terms are therefore relative. As soon as something is shared with another person (for example in a situation of accountability or confession) it is in one sense public even though it may be shared on the understanding that it should go no further and thus in another sense remains private.

Avoiding two extremes

In relation to the public/private distinction Christians currently face two opposing dangers that both need to be avoided. On the one hand, Christians can buy into the privatisation of ethics, particularly sexual ethics. This is prevalent in our society and views decisions in this area as nobody else's business. This then easily becomes an excuse for treating all matters relating to sex as a secret area of life which has no bearing on other people or other aspects of one's own life. This denies Christ's lordship over all of our life and our being members one of another in the body of Christ (a central theme in 1 Corinthians and its discussion of sexuality). It also erodes any sense of discipleship in the context of mutual accountability and responsibility.

On the other hand, some church communities can develop such a desire for purity (which can become narrowly focussed on sexual matters) or such an emphasis on authority and discipline that church leaders or the wider membership become prurient and invasive of Christians' personal lives and struggles.

Principles of pastoral practice need to avoid both these two extremes.

Connecting to the five categories

In relation to the five-fold categories used to understand homosexuality, issues relating to *attraction, orientation* and *sexual behaviour* are generally private matters, not publicly obvious. This means they need not be an issue of concern in wider church life unless they are made so by the person themselves or by others (through their enquiries, speculation, rumour or gossip). In contrast, a gay *identity* is usually – but not always – to some degree public (obviously so if it becomes political and campaigning). Similarly, *relationships* usually have an inevitable public face even if a couple may seek to keep the existence of their relationship private or the nature of it remains unclear.

Creating safe spaces

The private nature of our sexuality can be a particular struggle for those Christians who experience same-sex attraction. They often feel afraid, or even unable, to share their personal situation with fellow Christians for prayer, counsel and support. There is a concern (often sadly with some basis) that, if they do so, they will discover that what they share is then shared with others so their situation becomes even more public. The subject of homosexuality remains politically charged and an area of confusion and ignorance in many churches. Sadly, un-Christian attitudes and behaviour exist within Christian communities towards those with same-sex attraction. As a result, personal sharing in this area can lead to people experiencing hostility or being ostracised. There can also be rumours about their practice i.e. sexual behaviour or relationships. This is a reminder that in this area there is an urgent need to create safe spaces in our churches and for there to be a total commitment to respect for shared confidences. Although situations vary, much work remains to be done to put the first and second affirmations into practice in many churches. In the light of this challenge, the Evangelical Alliance has added the fourth affirmation to those made in *FHH*:

> *We encourage evangelical congregations to be communities of grace in which those who experience same-sex attraction and seek to live faithfully in accordance with biblical teaching are welcomed and affirmed. Such Christians need churches which are safe spaces where they are able to share and explore their stories with fellow believers for mutual encouragement and support as we help each other grow together into maturity in Christ.*

Official church policies

A similar distinction to the public/private distinction can be drawn in relation to the corporate life of any church. All manner of activities take place within the life of a Christian community but there are certain actions – such as ordination policies and authoritative teaching and/or liturgies – that comprise the public ordering and identity of the church. As the church is the body of Christ, and to be ruled by him through his word, it is vital that in these areas there is integrity and visible faithfulness to the will of God as revealed in Scripture. This is also important in relation to faithful Christian mission where the church has to act as salt and light in the world, bearing clear witness to wider society of God's purposes for human flourishing.

In the light of the third affirmation, explored in chapter two, which affirms marriage as the context for sexual relations, the Evangelical Alliance reaffirms, in affirmations five and six, stances taken in *FHH* concerning opposition to certain developments within the public life of the Christian church. These apply biblical teaching on sexual ethics to questions concerning the sexual behaviour of those being ordained [86] and the blessing of non-marital sexual relationships.

Drawing on the distinction made above, it is vitally important to recognise that the problem with such proposed developments is that of *practice* – 'sexually active' being the key phrase – and not one of *orientation*. The seventh affirmation therefore clearly commends and encourages those who live in accordance with biblical teaching and makes clear that those who do so "can bring invaluable insights and experience to the sphere of Christian pastoral ministry" and "should be eligible for ordination and leadership within the church". [87]

---

86 For a discussion of theological considerations concerning the ordination of practising homosexuals and representing a range of views see Rae and Redding 2000.

87 The wording in *FHH* was unhelpful here as "chastity" was defined in *FHH* (p. 17) too narrowly as "abstention from genital sex" whereas, as discussed above (especially in 2.1.3), married couples are also called to be chaste – by being faithful to their spouse. Also, celibacy was defined as "a lifelong, rather than a provisional, commitment to sexual abstinence" which commitment cannot be expected of "homosexual Christian people", as some may enter heterosexual marriage.

Chapter Four

Pastoral Practice for a Community of Grace and Truth: Sexual Attraction, Orientation and Identity

Affirmation
(8) We welcome and support the work of those individuals and organisations who responsibly seek to help Christians who experience same-sex attraction as in conflict with their commitment to live in accordance with biblical teaching. This help will involve counsel and pastoral support to live a chaste life and, as part of this process, some may seek and experience changes in the strength or direction of their same-sex attractions.

4.1 Setting the scene for pastoral practice

Using the framework and principles set out in chapter three and being faithful to the seven affirmations already made, this chapter and the one which follows explore a number of more detailed pastoral issues.

Approach with caution

As was already briefly noted in the introduction to chapter three, great care needs to be taken in applying the first three affirmations to specific pastoral situations. This is for the following reasons. *First*, as stated in the introduction to the affirmations, "We are conscious that different evangelicals might apply certain of these points in different ways." Any differences within pastoral responses to specific situations such as those discussed here is clearly a secondary matter. The detailed discussion of scenarios in these final two chapters merely offers guidelines. These guidelines should not be treated as of equivalent significance to the ten fundamental affirmations. *Second*, and related, evangelicals are found in a variety of denominations. Each of these has its own traditions, understandings and structures in relation to authority, pastoral guidance and church discipline. *Third*, every single individual and each church community is unique. It is thus neither desirable nor possible to give detailed guidance that can apply in every context. It is, however, possible to work with the principles outlined in the previous chapter and the affirmations which have been made and, in the light of them, to consider some illustrative cases in broad outline.

How these chapters work

What follows seeks to navigate various pastoral challenges by drawing on nine different imaginary scenarios. The cases are divided between two chapters on the basis of the two categories of orientation and practice, which were explored in chapter three (3.1). In this chapter there are four cases which are each explored in turn. These revolve around issues of orientation. Here it is assumed that there are no questions relating to practice that need to be considered. This means that the truth relating to the dignity of all human beings (affirmation two) is the primary focus here rather than the truth relating to marriage and sexual ethics (affirmation three). In the next chapter, where five new situations are described and then explored together, questions relating to upholding a Christian sexual ethic and a faithful response to homosexual practice in the church also arise and need to be considered.

All the scenarios are, of course, fictional constructions for reflection. Any similarity in content or names to any real situation is purely co-incidental. It is hoped that the scenarios are sufficiently realistic to help pastors, those in church leadership, and others to recognise the diversity of situations that might arise relating to homosexuality. The task, then, is to think through how a gospel-based approach – upholding the twin truths of grace and truth summarised in the second and third affirmations (of chapter two) – might draw on the framework of chapter three to address more specific situations.

Although guidance is given in a number of places, the extent to which it is prescriptive varies. Only some of the practical, pastoral implications are obvious and necessary consequences of the fundamental affirmations. The nine scenarios do not claim – even when taken as a whole set – to be comprehensive, addressing every possible area that could arise. Evangelicals cannot expect an answer book. We will need the wisdom of Christ and the discernment given by the Spirit to determine a godly response in each particular situation. By drawing on the wisdom of those with experience in this area and through reflection on plausible 'real-life' narratives, it is hoped that this chapter and the one which follows will be helpful for those seeking such wisdom and discernment in order to create a community of grace based on biblical truth.

Suggestions on how to use this chapter

To make the most of this chapter it is recommended that you consider your own response to each of the scenarios before reading through the reflections upon them.

Areas to consider would include:

- placing yourself in the shoes of the people described
- recognising any similarities in your own experience
- acknowledging your emotional reactions
- identifying and trying to answer the biblical, theological and practical questions that are raised
- responding to the challenges for the individuals described, their congregations and church leaders.

In particular, consider how a biblically faithful and Christ-like response may be developed on the basis of the affirmations made so far, specifically:

· the fundamental gospel focus of chapter one

· the twin truths of chapter two concerning God's love and concern for all and his standards for sexual behaviour

· the pastoral framework of chapter three, particularly the distinctions (a) between sexual attraction, orientation, identity, behaviour and relationships and (b) between the private and the public realms.

After each of the scenarios there is a discussion of some of the issues which are either raised directly by the situation described or are related to it. In the light of that discussion, you may wish to revisit the scenario and reflect on your own original response. It may also be helpful to use these scenarios in small groups and as part of your church's education or training in this area.

It is important to stress that the discussion of each scenario is not seeking to be exhaustive. Some people's situations may suggest issues that are only discussed in later case studies. In real life each of the situations may, over time, develop in ways that raise further questions that are not covered in the discussion of the case as presented.

4.2 Four pastoral scenarios

In this chapter, we begin by recognising that pastoral issues concerning a person's sexuality may arise because others raise them (the person is 'outed'), perhaps because of their concerns about the person's situation. The opening scenario explores this. In other situations, the person themselves is open about their sexuality (they 'come out'), whether relatively privately or quite publicly. The next three scenarios explore the different options and issues that can arise when someone makes others aware of their experience of same-sex attraction and seeks Christian support to live a chaste, faithful life.

4.2.1 Pete - being 'outed' and being in leadership

Pete, a single man in his late twenties, joined the congregation about two years ago. He has volunteered to be involved with the youth group and has been accepted after full CRB checks. After his first few weeks, Ian, a parent of one of the teenage boys, comes to you, because you are the person with oversight of the youth work, to say that he and a number of other parents are concerned. They believe that Pete is gay and they are therefore not happy that he is involved with the Christian care and nurture of the church's children and young people.

Correcting confusions

Attitudes such as those expressed here by Ian are regrettably still widely held, with some Christians unhappy about anyone who experiences same-sex attraction being involved in leadership. The concerns, if made specific, often fall into one of two forms. It may be feared that if Pete is gay he will be supportive of same-sex sexual relations in his teaching and mentoring of young people. However, as other scenarios below illustrate, there are many Christians who, while experiencing same-sex attraction, are committed to biblical teaching. This concern is therefore really not to do with someone's sexuality. It highlights rather the need for those with oversight in the church to be confident that those involved in Christian teaching, including of young people, will – whatever their personal sexuality – uphold biblical truth.

Another concern may be that Pete could be promiscuous or predatory in his sexuality and this is a particular concern where children and young people are concerned. This often signals confusion about the experience of same-sex attraction and sexual attraction to minors (paedophilia). Paedophilia is, however, a totally distinct experience: there are both heterosexual and homosexual paedophiles and most homosexuals, like most heterosexuals, are not sexually attracted to children.

Clearly any of these other matters are a cause for serious concern. However, there is no evidence of any of these problems in this scenario. If there is evidence it is such issues rather than a person's same-sex attraction that needs to be addressed.

This scenario therefore primarily raises a number of questions about both the conduct and the understanding of Ian (and any others for whom he speaks). It appears Ian's approach is a response to rumours about Pete's sexuality. These are then being used to question his suitability for ministry. It is important that those, like Ian, who have concerns feel it is safe to raise them privately with church leaders and avoid gossip. Nevertheless, the earlier discussion and affirmations make clear that evangelicals should not view a person's homosexuality as in itself any ground for concern about their suitability for leadership. Where it is viewed as such, or where it is simply presumed to be connected to forms of sexual misconduct, there needs to be re-education and a challenge to change attitudes and behaviour.[88]

Caring for Pete

Careful thought will also need to be given to care for Pete given these rumours. This is particularly the case if he is same-sex attracted and becomes aware of what is being said and done. The fear of being 'outed' is often difficult for those who have not experienced it to understand. It must never be under-estimated. One gay vicar (writing under a pseudonym) 'Chris' describes how he told a fellow ordinand, 'Michael', about his sexuality:

---

88 Churches and religious groups also need to be alert to recent legislation relating to employment where potential claims of illegal discrimination on grounds of sexual orientation are possible. Schedule 9 (2)and (3) of the Equality Act 2010 deals with relevant occupational requirements and the narrow exception which allows religious groups to discriminate lawfully in certain instances. It should be noted that official guidance to the Act specifically notes that "This exception is unlikely to permit a requirement that a church youth worker who primarily organises sporting activities is celibate if he is gay, but it may apply if the youth worker mainly teaches Bible classes".

I'd been living in a faintly evangelical theological college for more than two years and I was more than anything afraid of the consequences to my life, my ministry and my mental health if word got out that I was gay... I was still wrestling with all the voices from the past, the Midlands and the church that being gay was a deeply shameful thing... I remember the strangest things about it. I recall that once I'd said I need to talk to you, I'd more or less created a sense of gravity which could only be warranted by one of two things: being gay or being terminally ill. How surreal is that? Why should an accidental sexual preference come anywhere near something as serious as life-threatening illness? [89]

That struggle to be open with fellow Christians is also usually the end of a very long process:

You remember how much I had to beat around the bush before I actually said to you, 'Michael, I think I'm gay'? Well, that's nothing compared to the length of time it took me to admit it to myself. If I'm honest, I was well into my early 20s before I was able to talk to myself about it. It's quite hard to express just how unthinkable it was for me to be gay – or rather, just how difficult it would have been to survive healthily in my own head in the Midlands as a teenager – or later, in a thriving evangelical church – if I'd been that honest with myself. So to cut a long story short, I managed to keep the truth from myself for a long time. Part of me knew, but part of me was kept very much in the dark... There was an important hungry part of me that I was never able to talk about or even begin to make sense of. [90]

Everyone, particularly those with pastoral responsibility, needs therefore to be highly sensitive about any discussions concerning someone's sexual attractions/orientation. This is one of the areas where respect for privacy and allowing people to tell their own story in their own way at their own time must be absolutely paramount. When they are ready to

---

89 "Michael" and "Chris" 2005, p7.

90 "Michael" and "Chris" 2005, pp 10, 11. See also Hill 2010.

be open (or when they are forced into being open by the behaviour of others) it is also of vital importance that (obviously with the consent of the person involved) church leaders give them clear and public support. This is especially important if they are in leadership. The distinction between orientation and practice may need to be explained and the sort of concerns expressed by Ian addressed in order to counter ignorance or unintentionally hurtful comments or attitudes.

If Pete is gay and committed to following biblical teaching there will then be a number of new challenges about how he should respond and how the church can support him. The next two scenarios explore two paths facing those who experience same-sex attraction and seek to be faithful to biblical teaching.

4.2.2 Helena - seeking change

Helena in your church home group is in her late 20s. She has been open with the group about her struggles with same-sex attraction and her desire to be rid of these feelings, fall in love with a man, and get married. She shares with the group that she has discovered a new Christian 'healing ministry' which offers 'release' and 'wholeness' to men and women in her situation. She was bitterly disappointed when she tried something similar nearly 10 years ago when a student but she believes this is her best hope and that she should start their 12-week course of counselling and healing prayer for those seeking to come out of lesbianism.

Controversy and conflict – The background to seeking change

The attempt to diminish or change the direction of a person's same-sex attraction is perhaps one of the most controversial areas of debate about homosexuality in both the church and wider society. This is understandable both because some have principled objections to people wanting to change and because there is potential for damage if the attempts are coercive, make unrealistic claims or promises, or are forced upon someone by social pressure or stigmatisation. As a result of some of those features, and following pressure from gay groups, homosexuality was removed from the American Psychiatric Association's *Diagnostic and Statistical Manual of Mental Disorders (DSM)* in 1973.[91]

In a major review of this area published in 2009 the American Psychological Association acknowledged the range of different approaches to what it called "sexual orientation change efforts" (SOCE). It concluded that "there is little in the way of credible evidence" that could clarify whether any sexual-orientation change effort "does or does not work in changing same-sex sexual attraction". Nevertheless, it highlighted the need to accommodate clients' religious convictions

---

91   For a brief history of developments see Jones and Yarhouse 2007, pp. 35-7. For a fuller account see American Psychological Association 2009, pp. 21-6, at www.apa.org/pi/lgbt/resources/sexual-orientation.aspx.

and their right to decide how to respond to their feelings and behaviours in the light of these.[92]

As a result of the removal of homosexuality from the list of mental disorders, most professional psychiatrists have little or no knowledge or professional experience in this area. A number of psychiatrists, psychologists and other health and counselling professionals have, however, continued to offer therapeutic intervention. Their best known representative body is NARTH (National Association for Research & Therapy of Homosexuality). This is "a professional, scientific organization that offers hope to those who struggle with unwanted homosexuality" although its membership is wider than professionals and it does not itself offer therapy or counselling.[93] There are also a large number of Christian groups – many of them associated, in North America, with 'Exodus Global Alliance', based in Toronto or, in Europe, with LinC (Live in Christ) – which offer ministries such as those Helena is considering.[94] Although the models and methods vary, a common approach is known as 'reparative therapy'. This term is sometimes used for any attempts to change sexual attraction or orientation (often also called 'ex-gay' therapies or ministries). Strictly, however, it refers to a specific approach rooted in psychoanalytically-related models of infant development. It offers treatment based on the belief that "due to incomplete development of aspects of his masculine identity, the homosexual seeks to 'repair' his deficits through erotic contact with an idealized other".[95]

How then should Christians respond to Helena and those offering the sort of ministry which she is considering? Six issues merit further exploration here.

---

92   American Psychological Association 2009. For a response see Goddard and Harrison 2009 at www.fulcrum-anglican.org.uk/page.cfm?ID=475

93   http://narth.com/menus/mission.html.

94   http://exodusinternational.org/

95   Nicolosi at http://www.josephnicolosi.com/reparative-therapy-excerpts/

Christian freedom

First, it is commendable that Christians seek God's grace to be relieved from any desires which, if acted on, would lead them into sin. However, Christians who experience same-sex attraction should not be required as part of Christian discipleship to make use of programmes that offer to reorient their sexuality. Each Christian needs to discern whether or not God is calling them to seek any particular ministry or therapy as they seek to be conformed to Christ and live in accordance with God's will revealed in Scripture. Furthermore, the truth of the Christian ethic is not dependent on the extent to which people are able to experience a decrease or re-direction of their same-sex attractions.[96]

The question of causes

Second, Christians need to beware of privileging one particular model of the cause of same-sex attraction and developing a response on the basis of that model.[97] The question of causation remains a highly contested one with some claiming that a biological, or more specifically a genetic, cause has been discovered. They then further conclude that there is thus no basis for ministries seeking to help those who wish to experience a decrease or change in their same-sex attraction. This is, however, to go significantly beyond the available evidence.

---

96   See Jones and Yarhouse 2000 for a good discussion of the role of science in relation to ethics. One of the authors, Stanton Jones, has recently returned to this subject in Jones 2012a and, more fully, Jones 2012b.

97   For an accessible introduction see Yarhouse 2010, chapter 3. For more detailed data on biological factors see De Pomerai 2008 and on different psychological models see Harrison 2008. A helpful short guide is Burton 2006.

Nature and nurture

David de Pomerai, author of a major 2008 study[98] and Associate Professor in the School of Biology at the University of Nottingham, has written that "the claim that homosexuality is 'mostly genetic' in origin is scientifically unfounded". He notes that Bailey, the author of one of the twin studies often cited in support of a genetic basis, explicitly said that his work "did not provide statistically significant support for the importance of genetic factors for sexual orientation".[99] De Pomerai therefore concludes that the current evidence is that "there is no 'gay gene' as such, and media reports to this effect have been very misleading".[100] There may, of course, be other biological factors contributing to a person's sexual attractions such as hormonal effects or birth order. Here de Pomerai concludes that "The evidence for all of these biological 'nature' explanations is weak, but neither is it so negligible as to be dismissed out of hand. It seems more likely that different nature factors contribute in varying measures to homosexual tendencies, and that nurture factors play at least as important a role (possibly more so)".[101]

In relation to psychological models and explanations in terms of causes from within someone's personal history (not to be equated with 'choice'), there are again a range of theories on offer.[102] These include reparative

---

98   De Pomerai 2008.

99   Letter to Church of England Newspaper from The Rev Dr David de Pomerai, Associate Professor in the School of Biology, University of Nottingham, 9th December 2011.

100 *Ibid*

101 *Ibid.*

102 Stein 1999, chapter 8 surveys a number of these and argues that "there remain various reasons to be interested in experiential and psychological factors in the development of sexual orientation. Although there is little evidence for any specific experiential or psychological theory, experiences and environmental factors seem likely to be relevant in some ways to explaining the development of the complex psychological dispositions that we call sexual orientations" (p. 257).

therapy's neo-Freudian approach where the work of Elizabeth Moberly has been influential on some Christians.[103] It has been further developed by others seeking to understand same-sex sexual attraction as a quest to remedy a lack in same-sex parenting in which someone's desire for same-sex affirmation becomes sexualised. Others look to gender non-conforming behaviours in childhood as possible causes or contributory factors. As with claimed biological causes, the current lack of irrefutable evidence here does not mean that there is no relationship between the experience of same-sex attraction and a person's childhood, parenting and development. It does, however, signal that caution is needed in making any strong claims in this area and thus great care is needed in relating a particular theory to a specific individual.[104]

In summary, "It is likely that sexual desires and attractions are shaped and moulded in ways similar to other complex human behaviours, as biologically determined differences of temperament and personality interact with the familial and social environment".[105] The words of the St. Andrew's Day Statement therefore remain true that "the interpretation of homosexual emotion and behaviour is a Christian 'task', still inadequately addressed" and "many competing interpretations of the phenomena can be found in contemporary discussion, none of them with an unchallengeable basis in scientific data. The church has no need to espouse any one theory, but may learn from many."[106]

---

103 Moberly 1983.

104 The fact that in some cases people have sought healing in relation to an experience of sexual abuse or a damaged relationship with a same-sex parent and discovered that this has also had an effect on their experience of SSA does not justify claims that all experience of SSA has such causes or that finding some level of healing in relation to these other experiences automatically changes a person's experience of SSA.

105 Harrison 2008, p. 306.

106 Bradshaw 2003, p. 8.

Evidence for change?

Third, in relation to the effectiveness of sexual orientation change efforts (SOCE), many claim that these are discredited and never work. However, as noted earlier, even the American Psychological Association acknowledges "there is little in the way of credible evidence that could clarify whether SOCE does *or does not* work in changing same-sex sexual attractions".[107] Here it is important to recall the earlier discussion (see 1.3) rejecting the simple 'straight or gay' model and to remember that there is a spectrum of levels of sexual attraction to people of the same and opposite sex. There have been no high quality scientifically controlled trials on SOCE and claims for or against the effectiveness of any particular approaches must therefore be treated with caution. There is, however, plenty of anecdotal evidence from Christians (and indeed non-Christians) who have experienced a change in their sexual interests and attractions.

One of the better longitudinal studies of outcomes among people who enter programmes such as those offered by Exodus is that by Jones and Yarhouse. This study reported that "changes *away* from or the diminishing of homosexual orientation appear of larger absolute magnitude than changes *toward* heterosexual orientation". They conclude that "the general picture that emerges from these data is that on a number of standardized measures of sexual orientation, this population experienced statistically significant change away from homosexual orientation". Although the changes for the group as a whole were statistically significant, this does not tell us how meaningful these changes were nor whether some individuals tended to be affected more than others. In addition, this doesn't tell us *how common* change is. [108]

---

107 American Psychological Association 2009, p. 28 (emphasis added)

108 Jones and Yarhouse 2009 online at http://wthrockmorton.com/wp-content/uploads/2009/08/Jones-and-Yarhouse-Final.pdf. This is a follow-up study to their book, Jones and Yarhouse 2007. For their most recent work and responses to critiques see http://www.exgaystudy.org

Jones and Yarhouse's initial study followed 73 highly motivated individuals seeking change who were asked to classify themselves after usually at least three or four years in Exodus ministries. Of these, 11 (15 per cent) reported "considerable resolution of homosexual orientation issues and substantial conversion to heterosexual attraction" and 17 (23 per cent) said that "homosexual attraction is either missing or present only incidentally and in a way that does not seem to bring about distress". The largest group of 21 people (29 per cent) may have experienced diminution of homosexual attraction but were "not satisfied" and continued in the process while the next largest group of 20 people had experienced no significant change and nearly half of these had given up.[109]

Drawing on these and other studies, it appears that there is some evidence of significant change in the direction of sexual attraction for a minority of individuals. However, the most common outcome is either greater contentment in coping with persisting SSA or no change at all.[110]

We do not know how far these findings apply more widely. This is because the type of individuals who volunteer for studies such as this may not be very representative and the numbers are rather small. Given these problems and the lack of controlled studies, our overall approach therefore needs to be very cautious.

---

109 Jones and Yarhouse 2007, pp. 279ff. For a summary see Harrison 2008, pp. 317-20.

110 "Satisfaction and psychological adjustment to coping with the residue of SSA appear to be the main outcome. The group with the 'best' outcomes, that is those achieving diminution of homosexual attractions and marked growth of heterosexual attraction and function, appears to be 10–15 per cent of men and up to 30 per cent of women". Harrison 2008, p. 320.

Evidence of harm?

Fourth, as the reference to Helena's earlier experience and a number of respondents in the Jones and Yarhouse study illustrate, many people have sought to change their sexual attractions and been disappointed. For some, the experience has been even more negative with anecdotal reports that people have felt damaged by well-meaning Christians offering to help people seeking to overcome same-sex attraction. In some cases the response of Christians has reinforced stigmatisation or even treated same-sex attraction as demonic and requiring exorcism. It cannot be denied that in this area there have been occasions in which people have suffered from ignorance and homophobia and not been treated with the dignity they deserve.

Care is also needed in the language used. Language of "gay cure", "gay conversion" or "gay healing" to describe these interventions will be understood by many people to imply sickness or disease in ways that can intensify stigma. Promises of "freedom" from homosexuality are similarly inappropriate. This is because, for those individuals who do report significant changes in the strength or direction of their sexual desires, this is likely to be a movement along a spectrum rather than a "switch" or "liberation" from one category into another.

Recognition of the potential for harm and the actual infliction of harm in certain cases does not, however, mean that every attempt to experience change in sexual attraction will cause harm. As noted, many also testify to great benefit from such ministries. Jones and Yarhouse conclude that "we find no meaningful evidence that the attempt to change sexual orientation through the Exodus ministries causes harm".[111] Harrison's survey of the evidence concludes that more research is needed in this area because, although there are anecdotal reports of harm of various forms and people have attributed their mental health problems to these

---

111 Jones and Yarhouse 2007, p. 363.

interventions, studies in this area are few and of relatively poor quality.[112] Thus, because of sampling biases and problems in establishing causation, "it is not possible to generalize the chances of 'harm' to all individuals who may be considering entering some form of ministry or clinical intervention, although the case series studies suggest this is small". [113]

The need for good practice

Fifth, given the risks of harm, it is important that any Christians offering to work with people to diminish or redirect their same-sex attractions are suitably qualified and follow good practice. Those seeking such counselling and help must also consider such matters seriously. This will involve such matters as:

- compliance with standard ethical guidelines in such areas as informed consent, confidentiality, client autonomy and self-determination

- a clear rejection of prejudice and stigma

- care not to raise unrealistic expectations or make claims that cannot be justified by the available evidence.

A holistic Christian response

Sixth, as with so many areas of our experience where there are struggles and pastoral support or counselling is sought, we need to beware of responding to people like Helena (or Gordon below) in ways that compartmentalise or label their situation in a reductionist manner. A holistic Christian pastoral response should always be rooted in wise prayerful discernment and openness to the leading of the Spirit. This

---

112 Shidlo and Schroeder 2002 is the main study reporting significant levels of harm but Jones and Yarhouse 2007 points in the opposite direction.

113 Harrison 2008, p. 325.

will relate the presenting experience to the wider and deeper areas of a person's spiritual roots, history, wounds, battles and growth. It will relate all these to the need to recognise our human nature as made in God's image – created good but fallen and damaged by sin – and embrace the spiritual disciplines of confession and repentance in relation to sinful behaviour. Although psycho-social and emotional factors such as some of those noted above may be important, and knowledge in these areas is therefore valuable, there may sometimes be other, perhaps seemingly unrelated, factors which are important. Spiritual discernment and an integrated holistic spirituality are required if these are to be recognised and properly addressed.

Conclusion

In the face of increasing hostility from opponents, it is vitally important that Christians remain free to offer support within a responsible and ethical framework to those, like Helena, who seek counselling and pastoral care that will help them live in accordance with Christian teaching. The Christian Medical Fellowship's booklet, *Unwanted Same-Sex Attraction: Issues of Pastoral and Counselling Support* helpfully explores the various forms this could take and provides more details in relation to areas discussed above.[114]

---

114 Goddard and Harrison 2011b.

4.2.3 Gordon - living with same-sex attraction

Gordon, a member of the music group and an occasional preacher at your church, is a gay man in his late 40s. He left a same-sex relationship nearly twenty years ago because, a few years after becoming a Christian, he came to believe it was wrong to be in a sexually active relationship. Since then he has sought to live a celibate life though he has at times 'fallen'. Both his parents have died in the last year. In recent months he has felt incredibly lonely and struggled even more than usual. He is finding it increasingly hard to accept that he is going to be single and celibate for the rest of his life. Although most people in the church know his situation and history and he has suffered little direct homophobia, he finds very few understand him and there are even fewer people he feels he can open up to honestly about his situation.

Marriage or singleness?

Some who experience same-sex attraction will discover God graciously changing their experience and perhaps even calling them to marry.[115] This, however, is true of a (relatively small) minority of Christians who experience same-sex attraction. Most of that minority also continue to struggle with same-sex attraction within their marriage. The decision to marry is therefore one which needs to be taken with great care. It requires full openness about one's sexuality and deep understanding from one's future spouse. Failure to achieve this can arise because of being in denial about one's same-sex sexual attractions or because of the erroneous belief that marriage will end them and so they do not need to be acknowledged and addressed. Marriage in such circumstances is regularly disastrous with the person's same-sex attraction damaging or

---

115 Those who have such testimonies are often called 'ex-gay' or 'post-gay'. Among the best personal stories and reflections of such an experience are those of Mario Bergner (Bergner 1995) and Melinda Selmys (Selmys 2009).

even destroying a marriage and/or leading to sexual unfaithfulness with someone of the same sex.

For most predominantly same-sex attracted people, therefore, the biblical teaching outlined earlier means a call to singleness and life-long celibacy.[116] How does the church therefore respond pastorally to Gordon and those like him? Those who, at least some of the time, face the prospect with "dread – *the road ahead is too long and hard!*"?[117]

A supportive community

The first and positive thing to note is that Gordon is in a church which knows his situation and his history. He has taken the difficult step of being open and honest with fellow Christians. Furthermore, he has apparently not suffered as a result of this. A context where someone can be open is of vital importance. Wesley Hill recounts how he wrote to a fellow homosexual Christian:

> *I don't know if you've shared your struggle with anyone else, but if you haven't, you need to... I don't think I would have made it this far in my struggle with homosexuality had I not had the several close friends to whom I turn often for support, perspective, laughter (yes, it's really important in this battle, I think, not to get too heavy-hearted), encouragement, counsel, rebuke, warning – and most of all – prayer.*[118]

---

116 Keane 2001 contains a range of stories. Jeanette Howard's journey of seeking change and coming to terms with not finding herself able to commit to marriage is told in two books – *Out of Egypt* and then *Into the Promised Land* (Howard 1991, 2005). Two helpful short chapters exploring the personal and pastoral challenges facing people like Gordon are Roberts 2012, pp. 103-125 and Still 2006. A remarkable early evangelical discussion is found in the letters in Davidson 1970.

117 Hill 2010, p. 37.

118 Hill 2010, pp. 44-5. He admits "I could not have written those words in college because I hadn't told any peers about my struggle or experienced the kind of rich comfort and support I have since enjoyed."

This can only happen when there are Christians (and ideally not simply fellow strugglers but Christians in the wider church) with whom people can be vulnerable and feel safe. This is often not the reality. One of the challenges for many evangelical churches is that the way in which they defend an orthodox sexual ethic can sometimes make it more difficult for people to be confident they can be open about their own struggles.

Genuine friendships

However, despite this strength, it appears that Gordon lacks genuine friendship and support from among those who know his situation. This is a reminder that although providing a safe space for initial openness is vital and necessary, it is not sufficient. There needs to be an ongoing commitment to journey with people in deep friendship and fellowship, two of the other forms of love highlighted in Scripture alongside family and marital love. This is particularly important where someone is seeking to withdraw from networks or relationships which, while providing community, also led them into temptation and sin.

In one sense this is not difficult – 'Chris', the gay vicar quoted earlier, comments that "being a friend to anyone who's gay isn't hard"[119] – but it does require a willingness to listen and also to be vulnerable and open in return. In the words of his conversation partner, 'Michael':

> The support we give each other is nothing out of the ordinary... Basic communication really. I think it's also important to say that the friendship and support is mutual. It's not about me, the straight one, befriending and supporting you, the gay one. Rather, we support each other at those times when support is needed, whatever the issue or reason.[120]

That means that the friendship cannot revolve around one person's sexuality and that this issue must not be part of someone's agenda.

---

119 "Michael" and "Chris" 2005, p. 22.

120 "Michael" and "Chris" 2005, p. 22.

Having said that being a friend to someone who is gay isn't hard, 'Chris' notes that there are pitfalls – immediately checking up whether they are sleeping with anyone, seeking a 'quick fix', ensuring they know what the Bible says. These can arise in ways that would be unthinkable in relation to someone whose sexual attractions were heterosexual. What is absolutely crucial is listening and gracious unconditional acceptance without an agenda – "Accept one another, then, just as Christ accepted you, in order to bring praise to God" (Rom. 15.7).[121]

Brothers and sisters in Christ

An accepting community is important on a number of fronts. In relation to identity, it affirms that we are united in Christ, whatever our sexuality (cf. Gal. 3.26-8) and helps those struggling to focus their identity in Christ rather than in their sexuality or gay culture. As Yarhouse emphasises:

> *Believers who experience same-sex attraction are* our people... *I don't think Christians who are sexual minorities feel like they are part of 'us'. The nature of their struggle is tremendously isolating and there is so much shame involved in it... Shame is feeling bad for who you are. Because sexuality is tied to our sense of ourselves as a person, it is common for the Christian who experiences same-sex attraction to feel shame for their experience, regardless of their behaviour. What's the result? Often Christians who struggle in this way don't feel they are part of the Christian community. They often play the same tape over and over in their heads: they don't belong; they aren't good enough; people would reject them if they knew what was really going on; and so on.*[122]

---

121 An excellent guide to this is Tylee 2007.

122 Yarhouse 2010, pp. 157, 158.

Overcoming loneliness

A welcoming community and genuine friendships are also vitally important to counter what is a common experience of single people generally, but perhaps particularly pressing for gay and lesbian Christians committed to chastity – loneliness. Again and again the stories of Christians like Gordon speak of the pain of loneliness. 'Chris' writes of "loneliness and isolation... my loneliness isn't merely a social loneliness. It's a physical and bodily loneliness too, skin hunger – and not in a particularly lustful way either. I want to feel safe and held, to feel the assurance and warmth of a body nearby".[123] Wesley Hill, reflecting also on the experience of Henri Nouwen, describes how "loneliness... has been a defining struggle of my life. I think it is probably rooted, in a profound yet mysterious way, in my homosexuality"[124] and recognises that "coping with loneliness as a homosexual Christian requires a profound theology of brokenness".[125]

Deep and cruciform relationships

Creating a community of grace including those struggling with same-sex attraction therefore requires a theology of the cross and acknowledged universal human brokenness. This is then lived out in sacrificial friendship where we bear one another's burdens and so fulfil the law of Christ (Gal. 6.2). In our sexualised culture, such deep non-sexual friendships are increasingly rare and, particularly in relation to same-sex friendships, can often be the subject of suspicion. Churches, and particularly those in leadership, therefore need to promote, teach and encourage Christians to form and develop such friendships. This will mean being willing to wrestle with the questions and problems – including the establishing

---

123 "Michael" and "Chris" 2005, p. 23.

124 Hill 2010, p. 92. This is particularly explored in chapter 2, "The End of Loneliness".

125 Hill 2010, p. 118. For a powerful biblical reflection on this theme see Hays 1994.

and maintaining of healthy boundaries – that result. In particular, such deep friendships can help someone with same-sex attraction set their own specific experiences of suffering as a result of this within the wider experiences of suffering in Christian discipleship. Such fellowship can prevent their suffering becoming a crucible for self-pity and instead provide a context for mutual encouragement in Christian resilience and perseverance (cf. Rom. 5.3-5). There may also be recognition of shared experiences (for example of father-alienation and wounds from childhood) with those who do not experience same-sex attraction but who also seek similar spiritual growth and healing.

Discerning and responding to God's call

The church's call to deep and cruciform relationships is part of the call to solidarity with Christians struggling with same-sex attractions. This means the church as a whole needing to learn to take on board what is the given reality for those with same-sex attraction: faithful perseverance with what is likely to be an enduring condition that cannot be ignored and is not simply going to disappear.[126] This discipline of persevering through struggle is one all Christians face in some form. As the body of Christ, the church must also offer a patient, gracious and restoring response when people succumb to temptation and 'fall' in some way in their behaviour or relationships.

In such a context, Christians who are struggling in this area can be empowered to overcome shame and guilt. They can begin to accept their situation and even discern how it can be used positively by God for his glory and as part of their calling or vocation as a disciple of Christ and their gifting for the wider church (cf. 2 Cor. 1.3-7, 12.1-10).

---

126 The language of 'enduring condition' is used by Yarhouse, chapter 9.

The late William Still, a leading evangelical Church of Scotland minister, in his discussion of a pastoral perspective on the problems of our fallen sexuality, wrote,

> *Some of the most gifted people in the world in various realms have owed their God-used gift to the drive of sexual abnormality which has been accepted as an affliction (permitted by God, though obviously attributable to fallen human nature), to be to a degree sublimated, transformed and used to the glory of God....That very drive which could have ruined them was used, when transmogrified into an instrument of God, as the means of saving and blessing many.*

He describes how, recognising the tendency as "a fault and a flaw" to be put to death (cf. Rom. 8.13, Col. 3.5), God "will re-channel its drive, if intractable, towards something to be used by God. It could then become as beautiful as the fruit of those to whom the gift of natural union is given". God can transform and use Christians like Gordon "not only in the realms of artistic endeavour, but in those of loving relationships, especially in the befriending and helping of needy souls" and so the church needs to express "how sympathetic the Lord is to the affliction, and how he stands ready to use it when it is given to him".[127]

One of the best examples of this is the witness of Martin Hallett, founding director of True Freedom Trust (TfT). TfT is an organisation which offers "confidential Christian support and teaching ministry for men and women who accept the Bible's prohibition of same-sex practice and yet are aware of same-sex attractions, or struggle with other sexual and relational issues".[128] He has encouraged people like Gordon and the wider church to re-conceptualise our approach to struggles with same-sex attraction:

> *God has allowed our emotions and sexuality to develop in this unique way, in a sense, as our 'story' – God being the 'storyteller'. If we are saying our stories, including our sexuality, are not valuable, we are telling God He can create or allow something that is not valuable. If we believe that, it's hardly*

---

127 Quotations taken from Still 2006, pp. 61-63.

128 www.truefreedomtrust.co.uk/

surprising we doubt our own value. I believe we must accept our value, even if we don't 'feel' it – anything less than this is dishonouring to God. We can 'unwrap the gift' of our sexuality by accepting it, understanding it, and perhaps even hearing what God is saying to us through it. If we can see the value of the gift to us, personally, then it must be valuable to others, also. It can lead us to know more of God's love and forgiveness. It can help us to know and understand others. Of course, like many feelings and experiences, it can also be a liability and cause big problems for us and to others. However, nothing is impossible for God to redeem.... Are you willing to allow your unique story, including your unique sexuality, to be a living, functioning part of Christ's Body on earth? I believe, as we learn to know our own unique value, we can encourage our brothers and sisters in this way, also.[129]

In the words of C.S. Lewis, reflecting on John chapter 9 and relating its account of the man born blind to the issue of homosexuality, "our speculations... are not what matters and we must be content with ignorance... in homosexuality, as in every other tribulation, those works [of God] can be made manifest" and such an experience "conceals a vocation, if only we can find it".[130]

Conclusion

In response to people like Gordon, evangelicals, individually and corporately, need not only to uphold chastity and the sexual ethic expressed in the third affirmation. We must also take seriously the challenge of David Atkinson: "We are not at liberty to urge the Christian homosexual to celibacy and to spreading of his relationships, unless support for the former and opportunities for the latter are available in genuine love."[131]

---

129 Hallett 2000 online at www.truefreedomtrust.co.uk/book/export/html/69

130 Letter in Sheldon Vanauken's *A Severe Mercy*, p. 146 quoted in Yarhouse 2010, p. 181.

131 David Atkinson quoted in Stott 1998, p. 47.

It is to support Christians such as Helena and Gordon that the Evangelical Alliance makes the eighth affirmation at the start of this chapter:

We welcome and support the work of those individuals and organisations who responsibly seek to help Christians who experience same-sex attraction as in conflict with their commitment to live in accordance with biblical teaching. This help will involve counsel and pastoral support to live a chaste life and, as part of this process, some may seek and experience changes in the strength or direction of their same-sex attractions.

Groups and organisations working in these ways have an important educational and pastoral role and their experience and wisdom needs to be drawn upon more widely. There is, however, the danger that they can become a means of removing this issue from the life of the wider church and thus marginalising those Christians who experience same-sex attraction within their own congregations. It is because the Christian response to same-sex attraction cannot be left to such groups and organisations alone that the Evangelical Alliance has also made the fourth affirmation introduced in chapter three:

We encourage evangelical congregations to be communities of grace in which those who experience same-sex attraction and seek to live faithfully in accordance with biblical teaching are welcomed and affirmed. Such Christians need churches which are safe spaces where they are able to share and explore their stories with fellow believers for mutual encouragement and support as we help each other grow together into maturity in Christ.

The stories of Helena and Gordon have enabled us to explore how the church can support those who experience same-sex attraction along the two paths – seeking change and living faithfully in singleness – that fit with biblical teaching. In describing 'orientation', we also highlighted a third category in addition to the same-sex *attractions* which may be such as to amount to an *orientation*. This is the question of *identity* to which we now turn.

4.2.4 Iona – identity and family

Iona is a sixth-former and active member in the youth group who has grown up in your church. Her parents come to you in some distress because she has just announced to them that, as in the last five years she has only ever fallen in love with other girls, she has concluded that she is a lesbian. She says she is committed to sexual abstinence in line with biblical teaching, and is already sharing her faith with other lesbians in her year, many of whom are hostile to the church. They, however, are confused about how she can describe herself as both a Christian and a lesbian.

How should Christians like Helena, Gordon and Iona who experience same-sex attraction, understand themselves? This is especially pressing for those with strong or exclusive SSA who are unlikely to discover these attractions wholly and permanently disappearing: "but who do I say that I am?". Here, it is first important to understand why this issue of identity has become so important in wider society and then to consider some of the questions that must be raised about it, particularly from a Christian perspective.

Understanding gay and lesbian identity

In the face of a history of widespread social ignorance and exclusion, in the last half of the twentieth century those who experienced SSA developed a model of sexual identity. This is now increasingly on offer in our media and our schools as a means of integrating the experience of SSA into one's self-understanding. This model has been a major component in the normalisation of same-sex sexual behaviour in western societies. Young people such as Iona who experience SSA will therefore be aware of this model and, particularly if no alternative model is offered by Christians, perhaps drawn to it as the way to make sense of their first experiences of SSA which may be in the early teenage years or younger.

It holds that the experience of same-sex attraction is a pointer to help a person discover who they really are. This may be expressed in religious language in terms of how God has made them to be. It can appear as if same-sex attractions are to be viewed as central to who someone is as a person – they *are* a gay man/lesbian. This is especially so when this personal identity is strengthened through social and political solidarity with others who share it. This model is then usually supplemented with a call to find fulfilment by living out the reality of this identity in one's sexual behaviour and relationships. It can also be expressed through political campaigning for the normalisation of homosexual behaviour and same-sex sexual relationships.

This context explains why Iona is finding many confused by her insistence that she is both a lesbian and a committed orthodox Christian. However, the perceived incompatibility can also open up real opportunities to share Christ within the gay and lesbian community when committed Christians with same-sex attraction identify with them in a distinctive way and are open about their faith and supported by fellow Christians.[132]

As already discussed (in 1.3-1.4), one major problem with this model is that human sexuality does not divide simply and irrevocably into the two categories of 'gay' and 'straight'. It is rather a spectrum along which some people, to greater and lesser degrees, find they move in the course of their life. Particularly for young women, such as Iona, there are grounds to expect that she may experience some sexual attraction towards a man or men at some point in the future.[133]

---

132 This section draws heavily on the work of Mark Yarhouse, particularly Yarhouse 2010. More of his work is available from http://sitframework.com. Other resources are Tylee 2007 and Paris 2011.

133 A good secular study of this area is Diamond 2008. See also Dickson, Paul, and Herbison 2003. Good reflections from Christian women on their experience of same-sex attraction include Howard 1991, 2005; Selmys 2009.

Christian identity and sexual identity

From a Christian perspective there is an even more fundamental and theological problem. We earlier quoted the authors of the St. Andrew's Day Statement who stated that at the deepest ontological level there was no such thing as 'a' homosexual or 'a' heterosexual. Before that statement they had issued the following warning:

> There can be no description of human reality, in general or in particular, outside the reality in Christ. We must be on guard, therefore, against constructing any other ground for our identities than the redeemed humanity given us in him. Those who understand themselves as homosexuals, no more and no less than those who do not, are liable to false understandings based on personal or family histories, emotional dispositions, social settings, and solidarities formed by common experiences or ambitions.[134]

In summary, when it comes to understanding who we are, we are all liable to misunderstand ourselves. This applies to a range of self-understandings. It relates, for example, to our identity in relation to class or nationality as well as our sexuality. One of the authors of the Statement, Oliver O'Donovan, has explained its significance for gay identity in the following terms:

> We ask ourselves, 'who or what am I?' And the way in which we set about answering determines everything that follows... What, then, of a statement such as, 'I am a homosexual'? What status can such a claim to self-knowledge have? Clearly, we can't exclude it; we may come to understand elements in our emotional disposition that are properly, even necessarily, formulated in such a claim. But it has to be surrounded by a caution: such a claim can never be foundational or definitive. It may tell us something that is true about ourselves, but it cannot close the book on our self-discovery. It cannot protect itself against further questions and further answers. A knowledge of ourselves derived from our patterns of emotional response can only be

---

134   St. Andrew's Day Statement in Bradshaw 2003, pp. 5-11 (here at p. 7).

a provisional knowledge. It is part of the evidence; it tells us just so much, not the whole; and so it must be held in an open-ended way... When the Statement says, 'there is no such thing as 'a' homosexual or 'a' heterosexual', it does not mean that there can be no use for such a term, but that 'at the deepest ontological level' this distinction is not a determinant of personal identity. If one is conscious of homosexual or of heterosexual responses to other people, or, indeed, of both, that consciousness discloses a quality, like other qualities, of the person one knows oneself to be in Christ. It tells us 'what am I like?', 'in what ways do I function?', not 'what am I?'[135]

Different Christian responses

A growing number of Christians who experience SSA are recognising that this question of a proper, balanced perspective on the significance of these attractions is important in their discipleship and the right-ordering of their desires, behaviour and relationships. In particular, there needs to be a proper understanding of any sexual identity they embrace in relation to their identity in Christ.

As discussed earlier (3.1), some will identify as 'gay' or 'lesbian' Christians but without embracing the full package described above in terms of sexual behaviour, making their sexuality central to their identity or political campaigning. Their sexual identity will be placed alongside other identities – occupational (e.g. plumber), educational (e.g. graduate), national (e.g. Scottish or British), familial (e.g. sister and mother) – as valid and informative shorthand descriptors of aspects of who they are. Others, however, may reject this (along with the 'ex-gay' identity which tells a story of alteration of attractions and orientation) preferring to describe what is called a 'post-gay' path in relation to identity. One person on that journey describes it in the following terms:

---

135 O'Donovan 1998, p. 42 online at http://www.fulcrum-anglican.org.uk/page.cfm?ID=63

I'm post-gay because I chose to leave 'gay' behind. I chose to no longer accept 'gay' as an explanation of who I was and instead to begin a journey away from it. I chose to do so because I was convinced from the Scriptures that 'gay' wasn't a suitable way to describe myself, that it wasn't a valid way for a Christian to establish identity... Post-gay is a far better description for those who have left homosexuality behind. It describes a journey away from a false identity constructed around one's emotions and a true one constructed in following Jesus. For some of us that journey involves changes in our sexual orientation, perhaps marriage and kids. For others they see no change in their sexual attractions, but they have left behind the place of false-identity, of seeing themselves as 'gay' and that as a defining and unchangeable aspect of their being... Post-gay is quite happy to admit to a myriad of sexual attractions, but it refuses to be defined by them, not least because the Bible never refers to men and women as homosexual or heterosexual. Rather it is defined by a direction, a journey, a path towards God and his will for our lives.[136]

This perspective will have concerns about the common use and understanding of descriptors such as 'gay' and 'lesbian' in relation to Christians. It warns against an over-emphasis on them which exaggerates their significance and undermines a Christian's fundamental identity in Christ. It also reminds us that in relation to homosexuality, as with other areas, the primary calling of the church in her teaching and pastoral ministry is to establish all believers in Christ. That means enabling them to grow in their relationship with him and increase in understanding and faithful response to his call and gift of himself to them.[137]

---

136 Ould 2007.

137   A stimulating study of this whole area by an evangelical cultural anthropologist is Paris 2011.

Parents and families

Iona's situation is also a reminder to churches that those who experience SSA usually do so in the context of a wider family. Even if a congregation has no openly gay or lesbian members within it, it is now often the case that there are Christians in a church who have family members who identify as gay or lesbian. They too can face similar challenges to those described above (in relation to Pete in 4.2.1) as they consider 'coming out' to fellow Christians about this reality. Particularly when young people 'come out', the church has to help parents who are coming to terms with this news. There can be a range of powerful feelings.[138] These can include

- confusion, as perhaps false stereotypes of what it means to be gay and lesbian are challenged by the reality they know to be true of their son or daughter

- loss and fear, both in the sense of feeling the child is now somehow different and in relation to the different future that now opens out, for example, the lack of grandchildren

- guilt and anger, which can sometimes unhelpfully be encouraged if it is held that all same-sex attraction is related to problems in the upbringing of a child and their relationship with a same-sex parent.

There might also be a questioning or repudiation of biblical teaching, particularly if the child is seeking or is in a same-sex relationship. Pastors and others will need to be aware of such reactions and enable those in the congregation to respond in a Christian manner. More positively, Christians with gay or lesbian family members, by sharing their stories and new perspectives, can also be an important means of a congregation gaining a better understanding of the experience of same-sex attraction and its impact on others.

---

138 Helpful resources here include Yarhouse 2010 and Hallett 1996 (which is available free online at http://truefreedomtrust.co.uk/sites/default/files/Out%20of%20the%20Blue_0. pdf). Keane 2001 also includes some stories of the journeys of people – mothers, daughters, and spouses – whose family members were open about their same-sex attractions.

4.3 Conclusion

The four Christians discussed above have all experienced same-sex attraction but been convinced by – and are committed to living in accordance with – the view that homoerotic sexual practice is incompatible with God's will as revealed in Scripture. Despite this agreement with an evangelical sexual ethic, it is clear that scenarios such as these here do raise important and sometimes unsettling questions and challenges for evangelical churches if they are to be communities of grace and truth. The challenges are, however, even greater when there are situations in which Christians purposefully engage in homosexual behaviour and/or are in some form of same-sex relationship. These are the concern of the fifth and final chapter.

Chapter Five

Pastoral Practice for a Community of Grace and Truth: Sexual Behaviour and Relationships

Affirmations

(9) We believe both habitual homoerotic sexual activity without repentance and public promotion of such activity are inconsistent with faithful church membership. While processes of membership and discipline differ from one church context to another, we believe that either of these behaviours warrants consideration for church discipline.

(10) We encourage evangelical congregations to welcome and accept sexually active lesbians and gay men. However, they should do so in the expectation that they, like all of us who are living outside God's purposes, will come in due course to see the need to be transformed and live in accordance with biblical revelation and orthodox church teaching. We urge gentleness, patience and ongoing pastoral care during this process and after a person renounces same-sex sexual relations.

5.1 Setting the scene for pastoral practice

In the previous chapter our focus was particularly on the pastoral outworking of the first two affirmations which relate to the universality of sin and centrality of the gospel and the respect for the dignity of all people. These remain of vital importance and need to be upheld when considering the five scenarios introduced in this chapter. However, alongside them must be placed the third affirmation, that marriage between a man and a woman is the only relationship ordained by God for sexual relations, as that now becomes relevant to pastoral practice.

This means that issues arise concerning such matters as the need for those involved in homosexual practice to repent of sinful behaviour and grow in holiness. There are also questions about the nature of the church's ministry in encouraging this repentance and growth. In particular, thought has to be given as to how the church presents good, godly examples through its leadership, offers a distinctive witness, and in certain cases has to exercise church discipline aimed at restoring the sinner.

Approach with caution

It is important to realise that there will be a wide range of personal histories and situations embraced within those who might be described as, to use phrases taken from *FHH*, "sexually active homosexual people" or those engaged in "habitual homoerotic sexual activity without repentance" and "gay partnerships". In addition, there are the wider difficulties noted at the start of the previous chapter. There are, for example, different evangelical church cultures and denominational rules concerning such matters as selection of leaders and the nature, privileges and responsibilities of church membership. Such factors mean that, in contrast to the ten fundamental affirmations in this publication, what follows cannot be prescriptive. Rather, by reflecting on the different situations, this section seeks to highlight some of the key pastoral and theological principles involved and to offer broad guidelines for a practical evangelical response in line with the affirmations contained in this resource.

Suggestions on how to use this chapter

In contrast to the previous chapter, here we will not take one scenario at a time but begin with five different scenarios. Despite this difference in format, a similar approach to the scenarios is encouraged here as in chapter four. It would be helpful to take time to read the scenarios and consider your responses in various ways before proceeding to the chapter's reflections.

Areas to consider would include:

- placing yourself in the shoes of the people described
- recognising any similarities in your own experience
- acknowledging your emotional reactions
- identifying and trying to answer the biblical, theological and practical questions that are raised
- responding to the challenges for the individuals described, their congregations and church leaders
- the similarities and differences between the scenarios
- principles that will help you navigate these similarities and differences.

In particular, consider how a biblically faithful and Christ-like response may be developed on the basis of the affirmations made so far, specifically:

- the fundamental gospel focus of chapter one
- the twin truths of chapter two concerning God's love and concern for all and his standards for sexual behaviour
- the pastoral framework of chapter three, particularly the distinctions (a) between sexual attraction, orientation, identity, behaviour and relationships and (b) between the private and the public
- the responses to the scenarios of chapter four.

After the scenarios there is a discussion of eight key issues which are raised and of how evangelicals might respond in one or more of the situations. In the light of these discussions you may wish to revisit the scenarios and reflect on your own original response. It may also be helpful to use these scenarios in small groups and as part of your church's education or training in this area.

5.2 Five pastoral scenarios

(i) Oliver and William and their child

Oliver and William are a gay couple in a civil partnership who have recently adopted a severely handicapped child. They became connected to the church within the last year through attending a course for enquirers. Since then they have been regular worshippers. Oliver has made a profession of faith and William describes himself as still seeking. The question of his sexuality and what discipleship would mean for his relationship with Oliver is one of the issues that is currently a barrier for him. They are interested in exploring a service of thanksgiving/dedication for their child.

(ii) Karen's relationship with Ruth

Karen has been a member of the church for five years, since she moved into the area from university. As a gifted singer, she is regularly part of the worship group and has preached on two occasions as part of testing a call to a teaching ministry. She has never spoken about her own sexuality but in the last year in conversations with church members she has made clear that although she thinks sex should be for marriage she does not believe there is anything in Scripture that says it would be wrong for someone to commit themselves to another person of the same sex in a loving lifelong partnership. Her old college friend Ruth is becoming an even more regular weekend visitor and always joins her on Sundays in church. There are rumours that they are considering becoming civil partners.

(iii) Luke and Harry's challenge to the church

Luke and Harry are a cohabiting gay Christian couple in their 40s who began attending your church together six months ago when they moved into the area. Although there was some hostility to them as a gay couple they found a home group which was willing to accept them both. It is now becoming clear that they are regularly challenging those in the group and the wider congregation who hold orthodox views on sexuality. They are asking why there is a problem that they are in a sexual relationship given their commitment and love for each other. They are distributing literature from groups campaigning against traditional Christian teaching and claiming that those who say there is a problem are being discriminatory, prejudiced, un-Christian and homophobic. Harry has recently asked to be added to the rota of those leading intercessions.

(iv) Steve's single struggles

Steve has lived with same-sex attraction for two decades since his first experience of falling in love with a school friend in his early teens. Since becoming a Christian a few years later he has sought to live a life of sexual abstinence and also tried, with little obvious success, to receive 'healing'. He is open with a small confidential support group in the congregation about his experience. As a member of that group you have heard him in the last few years speak of his sense of loneliness and need for love. He has confessed that this has led him to a number of one-night stands and one very short-term sexual relationship that nobody else in church knew about. During this time he has also become increasingly depressed. He has now shared with the group that he feels that he needs to find someone to love and to whom he can be committed. He realises that, although he cannot see how to justify it biblically, this may well involve 'homosexual practice'. He believes that, even if not God's ideal, if set in the context of committed love, this is at least better than what he has known in recent years and gives him a way out of his mental distress.

(v) Sally's sexuality, marriage to Paul and relationship with Janet

Sally and Paul have been worshipping in the church since they married there ten years ago. You have been aware that their marriage has been going through difficulties in recent months. You now discover that Sally has fallen in love with Janet, a work colleague who is a lesbian. Sally has decided that she needs to move out of the family home to think through her sexual identity and explore that relationship.

5.3 Eight issues to explore

In order to map out the different issues raised by these five situations, what follows explores eight different areas. It is important to recognise that many of these eight apply to more than one situation. In addition, some of the situations require us to think through several of the issues before determining a response. Once again, there is therefore the need to treat what follows as a whole. Not every issue raised by a situation will be discussed in the text immediately. Even taken as a whole, there is once again no claim that what follows is fully comprehensive. Other issues will arise in pastoral reality and may even perhaps be relevant in these cases. Nevertheless, the eight issues discussed here should enable us to cover most of the relevant key principles that will need to be applied in any situation.

A guide to the discussion

The issues and scenarios covered below are as follows:

Issues to be considered	Scenarios discussed in relation to each issue
(5.3.1) The distinction between sexual behaviour and relationships within the general category of 'practice' described in chapters 1 and 3.	Karen and Ruth Steve
(5.3.2) The public/private distinction drawn in chapter 3	Oliver and William Karen and Ruth Luke and Harry Steve Sally
(5.3.3) The particular challenges which arise when someone is on a journey into faith or is a new convert and young Christian	Oliver and William
(5.3.4) The role of conscience – its formation and reaction to conscientious but wrong decisions	Oliver and William Karen and Ruth Luke and Harry Steve Sally
(5.3.5) Different attitudes to one's own same-sex behaviour	Luke and Harry Steve
(5.3.6) The demands of existing commitments when there is a same-sex relationship	Oliver and William Sally
(5.3.7) The nature of civil partnerships	Karen and Ruth
(5.3.8) Issues concerning church membership, leadership and provision of rites	Oliver and William Karen and Ruth Luke and Harry Sally

5.3.1 Sexual behaviour and same-sex relationships

As already noted in chapter two, same-sex sexual behaviour and same-sex relationships are distinct, even if often closely correlated matters. As Steve's story shows, it is quite possible to be involved in homoerotic sexual practice on an occasional basis, divorced from relationship. It is also possible to be in a close friendship or even civil partnership which is not sexual in nature, as may be the case with Karen and Ruth.

In working out how best to respond to these scenarios, the earlier affirmations and discussion, especially those of chapter 2, point to the need to uphold the following principles:

(a) Although there are important differences between promiscuous and relational forms of homosexual behaviour, "all homoerotic sexual practice is incompatible with God's will as revealed in Scripture".[137] It therefore requires repentance and renunciation. Although increasingly unpopular, this needs to be said in public teaching and private counsel with the same strength – but no more – as biblical teaching and counsel about other sinful behaviours such as gluttony or greed or gossip or inappropriate heterosexual behaviour.[138]

(b) Non-sexual same-sex friendships are to be encouraged and valued within the church but patterns of same-sex relationship which are understood as equivalent to marriage are problematic, given the uniqueness of the institution of marriage between a man and a woman.

There are also two principles of equity or parity which need to be upheld in all pastoral practice:

---

137 Affirmation 3 discussed above in chapter 2.

138 It may be that evangelicals will increasingly have to defend their freedom of speech and expression in this area as legal constraints are introduced in Western societies.

(c) On the basis that "monogamous heterosexual marriage is the only form of partnership approved by God for sexual relations",[139] homosexual misconduct is to be handled in the same manner as heterosexual misconduct.

(d) Close non-marital friendships, whether same-sex or opposite-sex, should be treated in the same way within the Christian fellowship. This means there should not, for example, be an assumption that a same-sex couple (such as Karen and Ruth) are more likely to be behaving in a sexually immoral manner than an equivalent heterosexual unmarried couple. Nor should there be greater scrutiny of the sexual conduct of those in such same-sex friendships. Similarly, cohabiting same-sex couples where both are same-sex attracted should be treated neither more leniently nor more strictly than cohabiting heterosexual couples.

This leads to the next distinctive feature which was first discussed in chapter three.

5.3.2 The public and the private

In these examples, only Luke and Harry are openly and undoubtedly living in what Scripture teaches to be an immoral same-sex relationship. Their public witness to and justification of the sexual nature of their relationship within the Christian fellowship requires some public response.

Steve

Steve, in contrast to Luke and Harry, is known to have sinned in this area by those Christians to whom he is accountable and in whom he confides. In a vital sense this is public as he has confessed to them (in obedience to Js. 5.16) and so is promised God's forgiveness (1 Jn. 1.9). In another

---

139 Affirmation 3 discussed above in chapter 2.

sense it is private and it would be wrong to make his situation more public. Steve's need is clearly for greater support and encouragement to strengthen him in being faithful in his discipleship.

Sally

Although there is no public evidence that Sally is guilty of sexual immorality with Janet, her separation from her husband and open exploration of an intimate relationship with someone other than her spouse is public. It appears *prima facie* incompatible with her marriage vows. The complexities surrounding her sexuality need to be considered, understanding must be shown for her legitimate needs, and she must continue to be assured of God's grace. Nevertheless, the principle of parity expressed in principles (c) and (d) above requires the church community to respond to her as they would to someone who left the marital home and began to explore a relationship with someone of the opposite sex while still married.

Oliver and William

Oliver and William are similar to Luke and Harry but they are not publicly stating they are in a sexual relationship. William (who is not a professing Christian) is also clearly wrestling with what becoming a disciple of Jesus would mean for his relationship. Therefore, although there are reasonable grounds for believing that the relationship is a sexual one, this will need to be handled in the light of the fact that Oliver has only recently professed faith and William is still seeking (these are issues which are discussed below in the next section, 5.3.3).

Karen and Ruth

Finally, with Karen and Ruth, there may be concerns that the relationship is a sexual one. Here it is important that they are treated in the same way as any close opposite-sex friendship. The possibility of a civil partnership and the public teaching role of Karen may justify church leaders, as part of the discernment process concerning her vocation, making enquiries to ensure maintenance of biblical teaching which requires those in leadership to be above reproach. It is certainly important that such relationships in a congregation do not deter church leaders from teaching about the pattern of relationships willed by God.

5.3.3 The journey into faith and obedience

The cost of discipleship

The situation of Oliver and William is one which is likely to become more common if the church is serious about sharing the good news with gay and lesbian people. It is important to make clear the 'cost of discipleship' and it would appear that this is part of what William is wrestling with as he considers his response to Christ's call. Sometimes it may be right that this is done in a stark, almost confrontational manner (as with Jesus and the rich young ruler). This should however be the exception as the emphasis in Scripture is on gentle restoration of those in sin, reflecting God's character as revealed in Christ (e.g. Gal. 6.1; 2 Tim. 2.25; Heb. 5.2). There also needs to be recognition that we are all in the process of growth in moral understanding and Christian obedience and that, especially when someone is seeking God's will in Scripture and through prayer, the Spirit can bring conviction of sin.

Welcoming into a journey of transformation

Affirmation 10 reiterates the call made by the Evangelical Alliance in *FHH* to welcome and accept sexually active lesbians and gay men. It does so with an expectation that "like all of us who are living outside God's purpose", they "will come in due course to see the need to be transformed and live in accordance with biblical revelation and orthodox church teaching". This transformation is, in other words, usually a process, not something instantaneous. This process requires others in the church to show "gentleness, patience and ongoing pastoral care". The affirmation is wisely vague as to what timeframe might be represented by "due course". This is only proper given the complex variety of situations and the awareness all of us have of how, in certain areas of our lives, we can, even as mature Christians, be slow of understanding and hard of heart.

In assessing any particular situation it can be helpful to make a number of distinctions within a journey into faithful obedience. Where there is a Christian commitment (as with Oliver here) there should, if this is genuine, be a recognition from early on that submission to Christ as Lord and Saviour means one's sexuality and relationships are open to His guidance and correction and also a commitment to obey. It may, however, be some time before someone genuinely understands and accepts biblical teaching about sex and marriage. Once that has happened, it should result in repentance demonstrated by turning away from what one recognises to be sinful conduct. This step applies the general commitment to living under Christ's lordship to a specific area of one's life when one understands the consequences of biblical truth. In this step there needs to be wisdom to grasp what it means in practice to implement that teaching and give form to repentance in restructuring one's own life. This, in turn, requires moral strength and courage to act in this way, even if it is costly.

While in some cases what obedience means will be obvious, in others (such as here with Oliver and William) there could be competing moral demands that make discernment more complex. Some may expect such a process to be completed within a particular timescale (for example, a year) if it is being taken seriously. Others may be less concerned with a definite timeframe and more interested in identifiable signs of progress. This is especially so when there is the need to consider other factors such as (in the case of Oliver and William) a shared responsibility of care for a vulnerable child. This is an admirable work of grace which is discussed further (in section 5.3.6) below.

If, even "in due course", there is no recognition of the need to change, then some of the other factors discussed below need to be considered and ultimately the issues raised in affirmation nine and discussed in the final section (5.3.8) concerning church membership will become pressing.

The role of the Christian community

It is important to acknowledge that while the work of conviction and guidance is ultimately a work of the Spirit, this cannot be left to the individual on their own. Throughout this process, the church needs to provide consistent but gentle and not bullying teaching in the context of friendship, prayer and pastoral counsel. As in Christian discipleship generally, at least one relationship in which there is a level of accountability, review and assessment of progress will often be of help in order to help growth in grace. Support also needs to continue after a person has – as in the scenarios discussed in the previous chapter – renounced same-sex sexual relations. Sadly, the church can lose interest at this stage on the grounds that a successful outcome has been reached whereas many challenges, such as those explored in relation to Helena and Gordon, remain. Once again, the church must of course also show parity in its treatment of same-sex and opposite-sex cohabiting couples throughout its pastoral care.

By recognising that this will be a journey and by accompanying people on it, congregations will best be able to support people like Oliver as together in community they seek to no longer be conformed to this world, but to be transformed by the renewing of their minds and to present their bodies as a living sacrifice (Rom. 12.1, 2).

5.3.4 The role of conscience

The discussion of a journey into faithful obedience for new believers like Oliver could be expressed in terms of the need for converts to have their conscience reformed and renewed by God's Word and Spirit. Such reforming and training of conscience is also required for those who have been Christians for some time. Sanctification, including intellectual renewal, is an ongoing work in the life of all Christian disciples.

It is important to stress – against a common individualist and privatised understanding of ethics – that simply because a person believes something is right or wrong does not make it so. Nevertheless, our personal convictions about what God commands and prohibits are vitally important. There are real dangers in not doing something only because others have said we should not do it even when we see no good moral reason to refrain. It is even more serious to do something we believe is wrong simply because others expect or require us to do it.

In responding to different pastoral situations, it is therefore important to get a sense of how the Christians concerned have formed their conscience and reached their conclusions. This means exploring with them such questions as:

- How seriously have they studied the Bible and how do they interpret the relevant Scriptures?
- What respect have they shown to the teaching of the Christian church down the centuries?
- How have prayer and Christian counsel shaped their understanding?

In the scenarios here, it seems that Karen is seeking to be faithful to her reading of Scripture while Steve is struggling with the pressures of his situation and how he can obey what Scripture teaches. It is unclear on what basis Sally or Luke and Harry have reached their conclusions.

Part of Christian friendship and pastoral care and counsel will be learning together and helping one another in the formation of conscience as we discern the mind of Christ. Central in this will be praying together and reading and interpreting Scripture together in order to hear and obey it. Where this practice is not central, the differences in understanding are likely to prove much less capable of resolution.

It is also important to recognise and distinguish two different ways in which some Christians seek to justify same-sex sexual relationships. There are those who disagree with traditional teaching but are committed to obeying Scripture. They still need correction from Scripture but this is a qualitatively different situation from someone who agrees that Scripture forbids homosexual behaviour but argues that it is nevertheless still acceptable in faithful Christian discipleship and to be accepted in the church. Such a position clearly places personal beliefs and/or contemporary society and sexual mores above the Word of God.

5.3.5 Different attitudes towards one's same-sex behaviour

The two scenarios where there is undoubtedly homosexual behaviour – Steve's past history (and possible future) and Luke and Harry's relationship – are significantly different in terms of the attitudes of the Christians involved. Affirmation nine distinguishes between those who are repentant and those who are unrepentant. It also refers to those engaged in "public promotion" of "homoerotic sexual activity". It is vitally important that these differences are considered in the response to any particular situation.

As already noted, those who are repentant require assurance of forgiveness and encouragement and support in amendment of life. Those who are unrepentant require prayer that the Spirit may convict and lead them into truth. There also here needs to be prayer for wisdom and sensitivity to know when and how other Christians – particularly those charged with church leadership – might speak in a way that serves that goal. Those who (like Luke and Harry) justify their conduct, challenge biblical teaching and push a political agenda within a congregation will also need to have their teaching corrected in some form by church leaders. Their actions may be so damaging and disruptive to church life as to require an appropriate form of church discipline to be exercised. Here, again, care is needed that this particular error is not singled out and that consistent actions are taken against those who disturb Christ's flock by promoting unbiblical teaching in other areas (for example pre-marital sex, financial dishonesty, disregard for the poor, abortion or euthanasia).

Yarhouse in his study contrasts what he calls "the assertive advocate" with "the sincere struggler".[140] The former believes the church's teaching is wrong and seeks to challenge and change it and those who support it. Yarhouse argues that such Christians need to be able to see the integrity of those they oppose. That means that those defending biblical teaching must engage with them in a manner of "convicted civility" that listens to their concerns and encourages them in their wider discipleship rather than simply focussing on this area of disagreement and conflict. Where, however, such civility is met with continued political campaigning and disruption of the fellowship this conduct will itself require correction and perhaps ultimately discipline. Someone like Steve is, however, a "sincere struggler". Such people, Yarhouse argues, particularly need relationships and teaching that provide a solid foundation in Scripture from which they can put their situation in a proper perspective and so be assisted as they persevere on their difficult path.

---

140 This is most fully explored in chapter 9 of Yarhouse 2010 which is drawn upon here.

5.3.6 The demands of existing commitments

In developing a wise pastoral response to people in same-sex relationships, there needs to be not only a focus on the individual concerned, but also a recognition of the impact of their actions on other parties.

Sally

In the case of Sally, there is the existing marriage and these situations are often the most painful, particularly where children are also involved. Sometimes a person has married knowing they are (or have in the past been) primarily same-sex attracted but believing that their love for their spouse will enable them to be faithful in marriage. Some of these will have been honest with their spouse, but sometimes their spouse will be unaware until a crisis hits. At other times, the experience of falling in love with someone of the same sex is a surprise to the person themselves. Whatever the scenario, pastoral needs extend beyond the same-sex attracted individual to the wider family (including the even wider church family) who will require help and support as they process what they are discovering about a loved one.

The importance of marriage vows and parental responsibilities here add further weight to the universal biblical prohibition on same-sex sexual relationships. A same-sex relationship can, however, appear highly attractive if subjectively the marriage is experienced as a constraint from which someone believes they need to be free in order to be themselves. Here the earlier discussions in chapter four about a proper sense of identity and the need for support in not acting on same-sex attractions are clearly of vital importance if the marriage is to be saved and to be a source of flourishing for all involved.[141]

---

141 Yarhouse 2010, chapter 7 explores the situation of a spouse announcing a gay identity. For a powerful testimony of a married man's experience of same-sex attraction see Anonymous 2002, online at http://www.christianitytoday.com/ct/2002/march11/2.50.html

Oliver and William

A quite different scenario – but one which also requires consideration of other and prior commitments – is that of Oliver and William. Here, there is the fact that they are in a civil partnership and adoptive parents of a needy child. Someone becoming a Christian in situations such as this one faces major dilemmas which are not susceptible to easy or blanket solutions. They present a real challenge, particularly for someone young in faith. On the one hand, they are called as a disciple of Christ to refrain from homosexual behaviour. On the other hand, they have an established and legally recognised pattern of relationship which will often have many positive qualities and within which there are responsibilities to a child that also need to be considered. The ideal goal would clearly be for William to come to faith and for them to agree that their relationship should become a non-sexual friendship within which there continues to be stability and care for the adopted child. However, this is unlikely to happen quickly and may be impossible. In such situations some would call for separation and the ending of the civil partnership with as little damage to the child as possible. Others, however, may see the situation as analogous to the situation in other cultures of a converted polygamist. There the church has discovered that an inflexible position (which required strict and rapid conformity to biblical teaching about marriage through divorcing all but one wife) was not always wise. Instead, Christians in such cultures discerned that, given the brokenness of the situation and the need to act in order to protect the weak and vulnerable, there needs to be a special form of acceptance (but not endorsement) of a form of life that initially might appear a 'second best' or a 'lesser evil' situation.[142]

---

142 For comparison of responses to cultures where there is polygamy and where there are same-sex partnerships see Sumner 2003.

5.3.7 Civil partnerships

Definition and evaluation of civil partnerships

The major difference between the existing commitments in the case of Sally, compared to Oliver and William, is that Sally is married and civil partnerships are not marriage, either in UK law or in Christian theology. Civil partnerships are a relatively recent development. Established by the Civil Partnership Act 2004, the first partnerships were entered in December 2005 since when just over 40,000 have been established (up until end 2010).[143] They are a relationship between two people of the same sex which is very closely modelled on marriage. Civil partnerships are, for example, prohibited if the couple are brothers, sisters, or in other ways within the bonds of affinity that prevent marriage. They also grant the same status as marriage in law and are increasingly viewed as, in effect, 'same-sex marriages'. However, because they do not require consummation to be legally valid and sexual unfaithfulness is not a ground for dissolution, they are not inherently sexual relationships in the way that marriages are.[144] As a result, some have argued that Christians could legitimately enter a civil partnership and remain committed to biblical teaching as summarised in the third affirmation discussed above in chapter two.[145] There are, however, other aspects of civil partnership

---

143 For data on civil partnerships see Ross, Gask, and Berrington 2011 available at www.ons.gov.uk/ons/rel/population-trends-rd/population-trends/no--145--autumn-2011/ard-pt145-civil-partnerships.pdf

144 For an accessible overview of civil partnerships and a Christian response to them see Goddard 2006a and Perkin and Perkin 2008.

145 The Church of England's House of Bishops were thus correct in stating "While many partnerships will no doubt be between gay and lesbian couples who intend to be in a sexual relationship, there is likely to be a range of circumstances in which people of the same sex choose to register a partnership, including some where this is not so.... The wording of the Act means that civil partnerships will be likely to include some whose relationships are faithful to the declared position of the Church on sexual relationships" (Church of England House of Bishops 2005, paras 12 and 19)

that make them highly problematic for anyone committed to that teaching. These include:

- their exclusiveness which means a person can only have one civil partner and cannot be in both a civil partnership and a marriage
- their lifelong intention marking them out from friendship generally
- their legal status as equivalent to marriage, establishing a family relationship and being an impediment to marriage
- the general perception that they are sexual relationships and viewed as same-sex marriage.

Evangelical responses to civil partnerships

Given the analysis above, the Evangelical Alliance has made clear that Christian churches need to be assured they are free from potential legal action if they do not register to host civil partnerships on their premises.[146] This issue was debated in the House of Lords in December 2011, when the government sought to give reassurances that legal action on grounds of discrimination against a church refusing to host civil partnerships would be likely to fail.[147] The sixth affirmation (discussed in chapter three) therefore makes clear that the Evangelical Alliance's position which resists church services of blessing for gay partnerships as unbiblical applies to civil partnerships.

This refusal to provide Christian affirmation of civil partnerships does not mean a rejection of those who enter into them. Churches, in ministering to those in civil partnerships, need to recognise the qualities of love, care, self-sacrifice, commitment and faithfulness regularly shown by civil partners to each other and to encourage these virtues in all loving

---

146 Press Release, 4th March 2010 at http://www.eauk.org/current-affairs/media/press-releases/churches-must-be-free-to-refuse-civil-partnerships.cfm

147 House of Lords, Hansard, 15th December 2011, Column 1408.

relationships. Those coming to faith in a civil partnership will seek to grow in these virtues but will also seek to order their lives in conformity with Scripture's teaching on sexual behaviour. Given the problematic features of civil partnership status noted earlier, and the likelihood the partnership has been a sexual one, some may consider it right to seek a dissolution after coming to faith. However, as a civil partnership does not need to be sexual and is not strictly a 'same-sex marriage', others will not think dissolution is necessary in order to be a faithful Christian disciple.[148]

Those such as Karen, who as Christians may be considering entering a civil partnership with a same-sex friend, need to weigh the problematic features summarised above with great care and consider the impact of entering a civil partnership on their Christian witness. In our society, and in most churches, there will understandably be a presumption that a civil partnership is a sexual relationship, just as it is assumed that cohabitation between a heterosexual man and woman or between two gay men is a sign of a sexual relationship. Rather than entering a civil partnership, therefore, it is better to explore whether what they validly seek for their relationship in terms of legal security, social recognition, identification of 'next of kin', inheritance provision etc. can be better secured by other means.

5.3.8 Questions of church membership, ministry and rites

In a number of these scenarios, questions are raised concerning the proper form and level of involvement in the life of the church and access to certain services. These include: can there be a service (of baptism,

---

148 In March 2012, the government began a consultation with a view to redefining marriage to include same-sex couples. The ambiguities surrounding civil partnership noted here would not apply to someone claiming to be 'married' to someone of the same sex. The Evangelical Alliance is formally opposed to the redefinition of marriage, which it insists is an opposite-sex institution.

dedication, blessing or thanksgiving) for Oliver and William's child? Is there a problem with Karen's involvement with worship and preaching or Harry leading intercessions? Deeper questions about suitability for baptism/ church membership and being a regular communicant are also often raised in situations such as these. Here the distinctions already drawn and guidance already given are vitally important.

Church membership and the nature and purpose of church discipline

The ninth affirmation is clear that, given biblical teaching as discussed in chapter two, "habitual homoerotic sexual activity without repentance" is "inconsistent with faithful church membership". There are, of course, many activities which require repentance from Christians if they are to be consistent and faithful disciples. As the opening affirmation reminded us, we all remain sinners in the school of the Spirit. Care is always needed that we do not find ourselves seeking to remove a speck from someone else's eye while having a beam in our own (Matt. 7.3ff). There are, however, some forms of sinful behaviour which are so public, shocking and offensive in the church and perhaps even in wider society (cf. 1 Cor. 5) that they require the public action of the church to exercise discipline (sometimes referred to as the "power of the keys" (Matt. 16.19)). This entails separating the body as a whole from those involved in such immorality. This is done both for the church's own integrity and witness and with a desire to lead the sinner to repentance. For example, in the scenarios above, were Sally to move out of the marital home to cohabit in a sexual relationship with Janet then some form of removal from membership or barring from communion would be appropriate just as it would be if she moved into the home of a male lover.

It is important to be clear that it is "homoerotic sexual activity" which is "habitual" and "without repentance" which is the problem. As noted earlier, that description only definitely applies in one of the scenarios being discussed here. What is practically entailed by "inconsistent with faithful church membership" will likely be different in different evangelical congregations. This depends on such factors as denomination and general attitudes to church discipline and membership. Some will understand it to mean "incompatible with church membership" and thus entail removal or barring from church membership. Others will see it as preventing admission to church membership but not necessarily and always requiring removal (on the grounds that, as sinners, all church members are to some degree living in ways "inconsistent with faithful church membership"). The ninth affirmation also addresses public promotion of homoerotic sexual practice as liable to disciplinary action.

Church home groups

In many churches, a separate but related question could arise in relation to membership in home groups. Here again there will be a variety of patterns with some groups being very open to any members, non-members or non-Christian 'seekers' who wish to join, in which case there should not be a problem. In other contexts, however, home group membership may be explicitly for church members. Church leaders may also wish to place newcomers in a particular group. Here there may be difficult questions to address. As illustrated by the example of Luke and Harry, some home groups may be unwilling to include those in an openly sexual same-sex relationship, especially where there is no recognition of "the need to be transformed and live in accordance with biblical revelation and orthodox church teaching" (affirmation ten). Others may feel able to incorporate such a couple, although problems may then arise if the couple seek to gain acceptance of their sexual relationship and are critical of those who uphold traditional teaching in a way that prevents the group fulfilling its purposes of Christian fellowship and nurture. Clearly here, as in other areas, if the behaviour of certain people puts the well-being of the church or home group at stake, then church leaders will have to decide how to act to enable the group and individuals within it to flourish.

In whatever ways such questions of church or home group membership are addressed, the principle of parity with heterosexual sin is vitally important if there is to be any credible response to the inevitable criticism that disciplinary actions or refusal of membership represents an obsession with this particular sin that in turn could be viewed as evidence of homophobia.

Church membership and faithful discipleship

Judgments in relation to admission to the church (whether by baptism, confirmation or acceptance into church membership) need to be made in the light of the fact that this represents a turning from sin and a turning to Christ in faith for grace to grow like him. It is therefore appropriate that questions about someone's commitment to obeying Scripture are raised and their pattern and direction of life are considered, especially when these are a matter of public record and concern. Questions of sexual conduct and personal relationships are obviously included within this wider context. A refusal to submit an area of one's life to the lordship of Christ is therefore a bar to admission. However, matters are often more complicated. The problem may be disagreement as to what such submission means (as discussed above under conscience in 5.3.4) or acknowledgment of weakness of will and a 'besetting sin' (as with a 'sincere struggler' such as Steve). In these cases, decisions will need to be made as to the extent someone needs to have understood and embraced Christian moral teaching and reordered their life in obedience to Christ before being admitted.

Stanley Grenz, for example, in discussing whether those living in stable same-sex relationships can be members in good standing with the church, stresses the centrality of personal trust in following Jesus. He argues that "the church... ought not only to minister to all but also to welcome all into membership on the same basis. And this basis consists of personal reception of salvation by faith through Jesus Christ together with personal commitment to discipleship."[149] The crucial question here is how much substantive content is entailed in "personal commitment to discipleship". This could be defined quite broadly in establishing the ethical conduct expected for membership of what he calls "welcoming but not affirming" churches. Alternatively, churches may insist that eligibility for membership is closely allied to acceptance of the church's teaching on sexual ethics, as expressed for example in the affirmations contained in this book. Depending on the practice of different denominations, these differences in relation to membership may then be reflected in such matters as sacramental practice, for example, eligibility for adult baptism or admission to communion. Here again there will be a range of acceptable emphases in practice among evangelicals and between different churches who share a commitment to upholding the Evangelical Alliance's affirmations on sexuality.

Church ministry and leadership

All Christians are called not only to submit their whole lives to Christ but to use the gifts they have received for the building up of the church (the classic discussion being 1 Cor. 12-14, written to a church which was far from perfect). All do this as sinners, but it is clear that those involved in leadership and public ministry in the body of Christ are called to be good examples to the wider body. This is particularly evident in the Pastoral Epistles (e.g. 1 Tim. 3.1-7) and has been an expectation throughout church history. That is why chapter three above reaffirmed the Evangelical Alliance's opposition to "the ordination of sexually active lesbians and gay men to ministry".

Discerning what forms of non-ordained public ministry in the congregation are similarly barred to those in sexual same-sex relationships is a more complex question. Certainly the fact they are living

---

149 Grenz 1998, p. 133.

in a manner "inconsistent with faithful church membership" means that, even where they are not excluded from membership, serious questions arise about their suitability for having any significant leadership or public ministry role beyond being a worshipper in the congregation.

Public ministries central to the church's life and identity and focussed in the traditional ordained ministry[150] – ministry of word and sacrament and oversight of public worship and pastoral care – would logically fall under the same expectations and requirements as ordained ministry. There are, however, a whole range of recognised ministries, exercising of gifts and forms of leadership and responsibility within a congregation which are more of a grey area. Here the best test will be how those whose lives clearly fall short in other ways (for example, living in a heterosexual relationship outside marriage or known as gossips or liars) are treated in relation to these ministries. Also relevant is to what extent somebody's involvement in a particular ministry undermines the church's teaching and public witness and the discipleship of others. In making decisions here it is important to remember the consequences that would follow from endorsement of sexually active homosexual partnerships by the church. Those experiencing same-sex attraction and committed to chastity would suffer the loss of support and encouragement of the Christian community in their struggles. In continuing to see same-sex sexual relationships as a departure from faithful Christian discipleship they would increasingly find the church, like wider society in recent years, becoming a culture that undermined rather than strengthened their resolve. The practical consequences of such a change in church culture for those Christians commited to biblical teaching is another strong reason for placing some clear limitations on public ministry by those known to be living in a manner contrary to Scripture.

---

150 Evangelicals have, of course, a range of views and practices concerning church leadership and the practice of formal ordination.

Issues of rites

Finally, as British society continues to see a reconfiguration and disintegration of the family, situations like that of Oliver and William and their child will arise more often. Here it is important not to imply the church's acceptance of non-marital structures. However, we must also not reject children being brought up within them nor prevent them from being welcomed and nurtured within the Christian community. Once again, different traditions will have different expectations and requirements. Two distinctions may be helpful here. Some rites (such as infant baptism or formal dedication) may require commitments from the parents in terms of Christian discipleship. Those living in a non-marital sexual relationship may find it hard to make these or the congregation may find it difficult to receive them as genuine. Other services, however, such as a service of thanksgiving and prayer for the child and for those acting as his or her parents, should be much less difficult. Drawing on the earlier discussion of distinguishing the public and the private in church life, there is also the practical possibility of offering a private service of blessing for the child (for example in the parental home) rather than a public one before the whole congregation.

5.4 Conclusion

This chapter has presented five pastoral scenarios where, in contrast to the last chapter, people involved to some extent in church life are in same-sex relationships of some form or involved in same-sex sexual behaviour. In some cases they openly reject the view that homoerotic sexual practice is incompatible with God's will while in others their understanding is unclear but, to varying degrees, their actions would raise concern among evangelicals committed to that view. These different scenarios highlight the need for Christians, particularly those involved in pastoral care, to understand each person and relationship carefully, responding relationally in a manner that seeks wisdom and takes care in its application of the affirmations to each person and situation. Although not claiming to cover all issues, the eight issues explored in relation to the scenarios point to a number of important areas. As shown in the discussion of these scenarios, several of these issues may need to be considered in any particular pastoral situation. The goal throughout must be to respond to people in a way that graciously relates biblical truth to the realities of their lives and bears faithful witness to the gospel of redemption from sin and the transforming power of the Spirit of Christ in the life of the Church.

Conclusion

In the same year that the Evangelical Alliance published *FHH*, Stanley Grenz produced the important book *Welcoming but Not Affirming: An Evangelical Response to Homosexuality*. This resource, particularly in the pastoral scenarios of the last two chapters, has sought to offer a similar vision to his in which evangelical churches are welcoming and accepting of all those who experience same-sex attraction including sexually active homosexual people. Evangelical churches are, however, not affirming of sexual activity outside marriage, including within same-sex relationships. This reflects the pattern of the apostolic church. Its theological rationale, rooted in the ministry of Jesus himself, is summed up by Grenz in the following terms:

> *All who would become the Lord's disciples and hence join the discipleship community must do so on God's terms, not their own. This entails being willing to leave behind old sinful practices – including unchaste sexual behaviors – so that together we might become a holy people. For this reason, the welcoming community that the narrative calls us to construct cannot always be an affirming one. Christ's community welcomes all sinners, affirming them as persons of value in God's sight. But like the Master who boldly commanded the adulterous woman the Jewish leaders brought to him, 'from now on do not sin again' (John 8.11), the welcoming community of Christ's disciples steadfastly refuses to affirm any type of sinful behavior.*[151]

To assist in this, the Evangelical Alliance has made ten affirmations and explored some of the practical consequences if we are going to live out what we affirm as evangelicals. It recognises that these affirmations will be worked out in a great variety of contexts and unique situations and this resource has identified and wrestled with a large number and wide range of issues that need to be considered in pastoral practice. It

---

151 Grenz 1998, p. 157.

has mapped out a range of faithful evangelical responses recognising that among evangelicals there will be differences in patterns of pastoral response but there are boundaries. It is important that pastoral care is principled and not simply pragmatic. Pastoral practice thus needs to be consonant with all the affirmations made here if we are to be faithfully evangelical not just in word but also in deed, in practice as well as theory.

Having begun with the gospel of grace, it is appropriate to end by again recalling that we are called to be a people of both grace and truth. This must be evident in our teaching and preaching and also in our relationships and pastoral care. Evangelical churches need, therefore, to be places where, in response to homosexuality, as in all areas of life, people will encounter the welcome, forgiveness and transforming power of Christ whose grace is a costly grace that calls us all to take up our cross and follow him.[152]

---

152 A discussion drawing on these themes is Goddard and Walker 2003, especially chapter 5.

Further Reading

There follows a lengthy bibliography of over one hundred sources, most of them published since 2000, which have been drawn upon in writing this resource. For those wishing to explore particular areas more fully, the following are particularly recommended.

General

The best overviews of the subject from a perspective broadly consistent with the affirmations in this resource are:

- Grenz, Stanley J. (1998). *Welcoming but Not Affirming: An Evangelical Response to Homosexuality*. Louisville, Ky.: Westminster John Knox Press.
- Dunnam, Maxie D., and H. Newton Malony. (2003). *Staying the Course: Supporting the Church's Position on Homosexuality*. Nashville: Abingdon Press.
- Goddard, A., and P. Walker. (2003). *True Union in the Body?* Cambridge: Grove Books.
- Peterson, David (ed.). (2004). *Holiness and Sexuality: Homosexuality in a Biblical Context* Paternoster Press.
- Goddard, A. (ed.). (2012, forthcoming). *Living Truth: Christian Faith and Homosexuality*, Gilead Books (provisional title).

A helpful guide from a position broadly consistent with this document and engaging with a variety of views is Church of England House of Bishops. (2003). *Some Issues in Human Sexuality*. London: Church House Publishing.

The best overviews including a variety of perspectives from different authors on a range of aspects of the debate are:

- Bradshaw, Timothy (ed.). (2003). *The Way Forward? : Christian Voices on Homosexuality and the Church*. 2nd ed. London: SCM Press.
- Groves, Phil (ed.). (2008). *The Anglican Communion and Homosexuality: A Resource to Enable Listening and Dialogue* London: SPCK.

Biblical

The most comprehensive study of the biblical texts is Gagnon, Robert A. J. (2001). *The Bible and Homosexual Practice: Texts and Hermeneutics*. Nashville: Abingdon Press. The author also has much helpful material on his website – www.robgagnon.net

A much shorter presentation of Gagnon's views in dialogue with a 'revisionist' reading of Scripture is found in Via, Dan Otto, and Robert A. J. Gagnon. (2003). *Homosexuality and the Bible: Two Views*. Minneapolis: Fortress Press.

Bonnington, Mark, and Bob Fyall. (1996). *Homosexuality and the Bible*. Cambridge: Grove Books remains a helpful short guide from two evangelical biblical scholars.

Bird, Michael and Preece, Gordon (eds.). (2012). *Sexegesis: An Evangelical Response to 'Five Uneasy Pieces' on Homosexuality*. Sydney: Anglican Press, Australia. A new book responding to recent liberal critique. See www.sexegesis.com

Scientific

The best overviews of the scientific evidence are to be found in:

- Burton, Simon. (2006). *The Causes of Homosexuality: What Science Tells Us*. Cambridge: Jubilee Centre.

- De Pomerai, D. (2008). 'Biological Mechanisms in Homosexuality: A Critical Review'. In *The Anglican Communion and Homosexuality: A Resource to Enable Listening and Dialogue,* edited by P. Groves. London: SPCK: 268-92
- Harrison, G. (2008). 'Unwanted Same Sex Attractions: Can Pastoral and Counselling Interventions Help People to Change?' *In The Anglican Communion and Homosexuality: A Resource to Enable Listening and Dialogue,* edited by P. Groves. London: SPCK: 293-332

A helpful guide to the role of science in the Christian discussion is Jones, Stanton L., and Mark A. Yarhouse. (2000). *Homosexuality: The Use of Scientific Research in the Church's Moral Debate.* Downers Grove, IL: IVP.

Personal Testimonies

Understanding the experience of Christians with same-sex attraction is of vital importance. There are a number of powerful, theologically rich reflections including:

- Hill, Wesley. (2010). *Washed and Waiting: Reflections on Christian Faithfulness and Homosexuality.* Grand Rapids: Zondervan. Wesley Hill is a young, single evangelical man who blogs at http://wesleyhill.tumblr.com/
- Selmys, Melinda. (2009). *Sexual Authenticity: An Intimate Reflection on Homosexuality and Catholicism.* 1st ed. Huntington, Ind.: Our Sunday Visitor. Melinda Selmys was in a lesbian relationship, converted to Roman Catholicism and is now married with children. She blogs at http://sexualauthenticity.blogspot.com/

A variety of personal stories can be found in Keane, Christopher. (2001). *What Some of You Were: Stories About Christians and Homosexuality.* Sydney: Matthias Media.

Pastoral

- Goddard, Andrew and Glynn Harrison (2011). *Unwanted Same-Sex Attraction: Issues of Pastoral and Counselling Support*. London: Christian Medical Fellowship.

- Tylee, A. (2007). *Walking with Gay Friends: A Journey of Informed Compassion:* IVP.

- Yarhouse, Mark A. (2010). *Homosexuality and the Christian: A Guide for Parents, Pastors, and Friends:* Baker.

Bibliography

American Psychological Association. (2009). Report of the APA Task Force on Appropriate Therapeutic Responses to Sexual Orientation.

Anonymous. (2002). 'No Easy Victory'. *Christianity Today*, 11 March.

Bailey, J, MP Dunne, and N Martin. (2000). 'Genetic and Environmental Influences on Sexual Orientation and Its Correlates in an Australian Twin Sample'. *Journal of Personality and Social Psychology* 78: 524-36.

Bergner, Mario. (1995). *Setting Love in Order*. Crowborough: Monarch.

Bonnington, Mark, and Bob Fyall. (1996). *Homosexuality and the Bible*. Cambridge: Grove Books.

Bradshaw, Timothy (ed.). (2003). *The Way Forward? : Christian Voices on Homosexuality and the Church*. 2nd ed. London: SCM Press.

Brandon, Guy. (2009). *Just Sex: Is It Ever Just Sex?* Nottingham: Inter-Varsity Press.

———. (2011). 'Free Sex: Who Pays? - Moral Hazard and Sexual Ethics'. *Cambridge Papers* 20 (4).

Brooten, Bernadette J. (1996). *Love between Women: Early Christian Responses to Female Homoeroticism*. Chicago: University of Chicago Press.

Burton, Simon. (2006). *The Causes of Homosexuality: What Science Tells Us*. Cambridge: Jubilee Centre.

Chalke, Steve, and Alan Mann. (2010). *Different Eyes: The Art of Living Beautifully*. Grand Rapids, Michigan: Zondervan.

Church of England House of Bishops. (2003). *Some Issues in Human Sexuality*. London: Church House Publishing.

———. (2005). Civil Partnerships - a Pastoral Statement from the House of Bishops of the Church of England.

Danylak, Barry. (2007). *A Biblical Theology of Singleness*. Cambridge: Grove Books.

———. (2010). *Redeeming Singleness: How the Storyline of Scripture Affirms the Single Life*. Wheaton, Ill.: Crossway.

Davidson, Alex. (1970). *The Returns of Love: Letters of a Christian Homosexual:* London: Inter-Varsity Press.

Davidson, Richard M. (2007). *Flame of Yahweh: Sexuality in the Old Testament*. Peabody, Mass.: Hendrickson Publishers.

De Pomerai, D. (2008). 'Biological Mechanisms in Homosexuality: A Critical Review'. *In The Anglican Communion and Homosexuality: A Resource to Enable Listening and Dialogue*, edited by P. Groves. London: SPCK: 268-92

Deshpande, Lakshmi. (2001). *Singled out or One in the Body?: An Exploration of Singleness in the Church Today*. Cambridge: Grove Books.

Diamond, Lisa M. (2008). *Sexual Fluidity: Understanding Women's Love and Desire*. Cambridge, Mass.: Harvard University Press.

Dickson, N, C Paul, and P Herbison. (2003). 'Same-Sex Attraction in a Birth Cohort: Prevalence and Persistence in Early Adulthood'. *Social Science & Medicine* 56 (8): 1607-1615.

Dunnam, Maxie D., and H. Newton Malony. (2003). *Staying the Course: Supporting the Church's Position on Homosexuality*. Nashville: Abingdon Press.

Evangelical Alliance's Commission on Unity and Truth among Evangelicals (ACUTE). (1998). *Faith, Hope and Homosexuality*. Carlisle: Paternoster Press.

Evangelical Alliance. (2011a). *21st Century Evangelicals (Data Report)*: Evangelical Alliance and Christian Research.

———. (2011b). *21st Century Evangelicals: A Snapshot of the Beliefs and Habits of Evangelical Christians in the UK*: Evangelical Alliance and Christian Research.

Evangelical Alliance Policy Commission. (2000). *Transsexuality:* Paternoster Press.

France, R. T. (2000). *A Slippery Slope?: The Ordination of Women and Homosexual Practice: A Case Study in Biblical Interpretation*. Cambridge: Grove Books.

Gagnon, Robert A. J. (2001). *The Bible and Homosexual Practice: Texts and Hermeneutics*. Nashville: Abingdon Press.

Gates, Gary J. (2011). 'How Many People Are Lesbian, Gay, Bisexual, and Transgender?': The Williams Institute.

Goddard, A. (2006a). *Friends, Partners or Spouses? The Civil Partnership Act and Christian Witness, Grove Ethics 141.* Cambridge: Grove Books.

———. (2006b). 'Homophobia'. http://www.fulcrum-anglican.org.uk/?108

Goddard, A., and G. Harrison. (2009). 'Changing Sexual Orientation and Identity? A Critique of the APA Report'. http://www.fulcrum-anglican.org. uk/?475.

———. (2011a). 'Now for the 'B' Picture'. *Church Times*, December 9th.

———. (2011b). *Unwanted Same-Sex Attraction: Issues of Pastoral and Counselling Support.* London: Christian Medical Fellowship.

Goddard, A., and P. Walker. (2003). *True Union in the Body?* Cambridge: Grove Books.

Goldingay, John. (2010). *Key Questions About Christian Faith: Old Testament Answers.* Grand Rapids, MI.: Baker Academic.

Grabowski, John S. (2003). *Sex and Virtue: An Introduction to Sexual Ethics.* Washington, D.C.: Catholic University of America Press.

Grenz, Stanley J. (1998). *Welcoming but Not Affirming: An Evangelical Response to Homosexuality.* Louisville, Ky.: Westminster John Knox Press.

Grimsrud, Ted, and Mark Nation. (2008). *Reasoning Together: A Conversation on Homosexuality.* Scottdale, Pa.: Herald Press.

Groves, Phil (ed.). (2008). *The Anglican Communion and Homosexuality: A Resource to Enable Listening and Dialogue* London: SPCK

Hallett, Martin. (1996). *Out of the Blue: Homosexuality and the Family.* London: Hodder & Stoughton.

———. (2000). 'Sexuality - a Gift from God?' *True Freedom Trust.*

Harrison, G. (2008). 'Unwanted Same Sex Attractions: Can Pastoral and Counselling Interventions Help People to Change?' In *The Anglican Communion and Homosexuality: A Resource to Enable Listening and Dialogue*, edited by P. Groves. London: SPCK: 293-332

Hays, Richard B. (1986). 'Relations Natural and Unnatural: A Response to John Boswell's Exegesis of Romans 1'. *Journal of Religious Ethics* 14 (1): 184-215.

———. (1994). 'Awaiting the Redemption of Our Bodies: The Witness of Scripture Concerning Homosexuality'. In *Homosexuality in the Church: Both Sides of the Debate*, edited by J. S. Siker. Louisville, Kentucky: Westminster John Knox Press: 3-17

———. (1996). *The Moral Vision of the New Testament: A Contemporary Introduction to New Testament Ethics.* New York: Harper Collins.

Hilborn, David. (1994). 'For the Procreation of Children'. In *As Man and Woman Made: Theological Reflections on Marriage,* edited by S. Durber. London: The United Reformed Church: 22-32

———. (2002). 'Homosexuality, Covenant and Grace in the Writings of Rowan Williams: An Evangelical Response'. *Anvil 20* (4): 263-75.

———. (2003). 'Homosexuality and Scripture'. In *Growing into God: Exploring Our Call to Grow into God's Image and Likeness,* edited by J. Mayland: Churches Together in Britain and Ireland: 159-69

Hill, Wesley. (2010). *Washed and Waiting: Reflections on Christian Faithfulness and Homosexuality.* Grand Rapids: Zondervan.

Holmes, Stephen R. (2002). *Listening to the Past: The Place of Tradition in Theology.* Carlisle: Paternoster.

Howard, Jeanette. (1991). *Out of Egypt: One Woman's Journey out of Lesbianism.* London: Monarch.

———. (2005). *Into the Promised Land: Beyond the Lesbian Struggle.* Oxford: Monarch.

Humphrey, Edith. (2003). 'Same-Sex Eroticism and the Church: Classical Approaches and Responses'. *In The Homosexuality Debate: Faith Seeking Understanding,* edited by C. S. Hamilton. Toronto: Anglican Book Centre: 37-94

Joloza, Theodore, Joanne Evans, Rachel O'Brien, and Angela Potter-Collins. (2010). *Measuring Sexual Identity: An Evaluation Report.* London: Office for National Statistics.

Jones, Stanton L. (2012a). 'Same-Sex Science: The Social Sciences Cannot Settle the Moral Status of Homosexuality'. In *Embracing Truth: Homosexuality and the Word of God*, edited by D. W. Torrance and J. Stein: Handsel Press: 20-32. Available from http://www.firstthings.com/article/2012/01/same-sex-science

————. (2012b). *Sexual Orientation and Reason: On the Implications of False Beliefs About Homosexuality.* Available from http://www.wheaton.edu/CACE/CACE-Print-Resources/Articles.

Jones, Stanton L., and Mark A. Yarhouse. (2000). *Homosexuality: The Use of Scientific Research in the Church's Moral Debate.* Downers Grove, Ill: IVP.

————. (2007). *Ex-Gays?: A Longitudinal Study of Religiously Mediated Change in Sexual Orientation.* Downers Grove, Ill.: IVP Academic.

————. (2009). 'Ex gays?: an extended longitudinal study of attempted religiously mediated change in sexual orientation.' APA Convention: Paper presented at Sexual Orientation and Faith Traditions Symposium.

Keane, Christopher. (2001). *What Some of You Were: Stories About Christians and Homosexuality.* Sydney: Matthias Media.

Knight, George W. (1992). *The Pastoral Epistles: A Commentary on the Greek Text.* Grand Rapids, Mich.: W.B. Eerdmans.

Kuehne, Dale S. (2009). *Sex and the iWorld: Rethinking Relationship Beyond an Age of Individualism.* Grand Rapids, Mich.: Baker Academic.

Marin, Andrew P. (2009a). *Love Is an Orientation : Elevating the Conversation with the Gay Community.* Downers Grove, Ill.: IVP Books.

————. (2009b). 'Mission and the Gay Community'. *Anvil* 26 (3&4): 271-85.

"Michael" and "Chris". (2005). *A Gay-Straight Christian Dialogue, Grove Pastoral Series 104.* Cambridge: Grove Books.

Moberly, Elizabeth R. (1983). *Homosexuality: A New Christian Ethic.* Cambridge: James Clarke.

Nissinen, Martti. (1998). *Homoeroticism in the Biblical World: A Historical Perspective.* Minneapolis, Minn.: Fortress Press.

Nolland, John. (2009). 'Sexual Ethics and the Jesus of the Gospels'. *Anvil* 26 (1): 21-30.

O'Donovan, Oliver. (1998). 'Reading the St. Andrew's Day Statement'. *In Anglican Life and Witness: A Reader for the Lambeth Conference of Anglican Bishops 1998*, edited by C. Sugden and V. Samuel. London: SPCK: 38-51

Ould, Peter. (2007). 'You and Me Together'. Online at www.peter-ould. net/2007/04/19/you-and-me-together/.

Paris, Jenell Williams. (2011). *The End of Sexual Identity: Why Sex Is Too Important to Define Who We Are*. Downers Grove, Ill.: IVP Books.

Perkin, Paul, and Christine Perkin. (2008). 'Civil Partnerships - Advice to UK Parishes and Clergy'. In *God, Gays and the Church,* edited by L. Nolland, C. Sugden and S. Finch. London: Latimer Trust: 165-75

Peterson, David (ed.). (2004). *Holiness and Sexuality: Homosexuality in a Biblical Context*: Paternoster Press.

Rae, Murray, and Graham Redding, eds. (2000). *More Than a Single Issue: Theological Considerations Concerning the Ordination of Practising Homosexuals.* Adelaide: Openbook.

Riley, Patrick. (2000). *Civilizing Sex: On Chastity and the Common Good.* Edinburgh: T&T Clark.

Roberts, Christopher Chenault. (2007). *Creation and Covenant: The Significance of Sexual Difference in and for the Moral Theology of Marriage.* London: T & T Clark.

Roberts, Vaughan. (2012). *Battles Christians Face*. Milton Keynes: Authentic Media.

Rogers, Jack Bartlett. (2009). *Jesus, the Bible, and Homosexuality: Explode the Myths, Heal the Church.* Rev. and expanded ed. Louisville, Ky.: Westminster John Knox Press.

Ross, Helen, Karen Gask, and Ann Berrington. (2011). *Civil Partnerships Five Years On.* Vol. Population Trends No 145: Office of National Statistics,.

Sanlon, Peter. (2010). *Plastic People: How Queer Theory Is Changing Us.* London: Latimer Trust.

Satlow, Michael L. (1995). *Tasting the Dish: Rabbinic Rhetorics of Sexuality, Brown Judaic Studies.* Atlanta, Ga.: Scholars Press.

Savin-Williams, Ritch C. (2005). *The New Gay Teenager.* Cambridge, Mass.: Harvard University Press.

Schmidt, Thomas E. (1995). *Straight & Narrow?: Compassion & Clarity in the Homosexuality Debate.* Leicester: Inter-Varsity.

Scott, Kevin F. (2004). *At Variance: The Church's Argument against Homosexual Conduct.* Edinburgh: Dunedin Academic Press.

Searle, David, ed. (2006). *Truth and Love in a Sexually Disordered World.* Fearn, Ross-shire: Christian Focus.

Seitz, Christopher. (2000). 'Sexuality and Scripture's Plain Sense: The Christian Community and the Law of God'. In *Homosexuality, Science, and the 'Plain Sense' of Scripture,* edited by D. Blach. Grand Rapids: Eerdmans: 177-96

Selmys, Melinda. (2009). *Sexual Authenticity: An Intimate Reflection on Homosexuality and Catholicism.* Huntington, Ind.: Our Sunday Visitor.

Shidlo, A, and M Schroeder. (2002). 'Changing Sexual Orientation: A Consumers' Report'. *Professional Psychology: Research and Practice* 33: 249-259.

Simon, Caroline J. (2012). *Bringing Sex into Focus.* Downers Grove, Ill: IVP.
Smith, Mark D. (1996). 'Ancient Bisexuality and the Interpretation of Romans 1.26, 27'. *Journal of the American Academy of Religion* 64: 223-54.

Stein, Edward. (1999). *The Mismeasure of Desire: The Science, Theory, and Ethics of Sexual Orientation.* Oxford: Oxford University Press.

Still, William. (2006). 'A Pastoral Perspective on the Problems of Our Fallen Sexuality'. In *Truth and Love in a Sexually Disordered World,* edited by D. Searle. Fearn, Ross-shire: Christian Focus: 46-64

Stott, John R. W. (1998). *Same Sex Partnerships? : A Christian Contribution to Contemporary Debate.* London: Marshall Pickering.

Sumner, George. (2003). '"Patience Leads to Character": The Polygamy-Homosexuality Analogy in Contemporary Debate'. In *The Homosexuality Debate: Faith Seeking Understanding,* edited by C. S. Hamilton. Toronto: Anglican Book Centre: 216-26

Swartley, Willard M. (1983). *Slavery, Sabbath, War and Women: Case Issues in Biblical Interpretation*. Scottdale, Pa.: Herald Press.

————. (2003). *Homosexuality: Biblical Interpretation and Moral Discernment*. Scottdale, Pa.: Herald Press.

Taylor, Jenny. (2008). *A Wild Constraint: The Case for Chastity*. London: Continuum.

Torrance, David W., and Jock Stein, eds. (2012). *Embracing Truth: Homosexuality and the Word of God:* Handsel Press. Resources including digest and study guide at http://www.handselpress.org.uk/

Tylee, A. (2007). *Walking with Gay Friends: A Journey of Informed Compassion*. Leicester: IVP.

Vasey, Michael. (1995). *Strangers and Friends: A New Exploration of Homosexuality and the Bible*. London: Hodder & Stoughton.

Via, Dan Otto, and Robert A. J. Gagnon. (2003). *Homosexuality and the Bible: Two Views*. Minneapolis: Fortress Press.

Webb, William J. (2001). *Slaves, Women & Homosexuals: Exploring the Hermeneutics of Cultural Analysis*. Downers Grove, Ill.: InterVarsity Press.

————. (2004). 'Gender Equality and Homosexuality'. In *Discovering Biblical Equality: Complementarity without Hierarchy*, edited by R. W. Pierce and R. M. Groothuis. Leicester: IVP Apollos: 401-13

Williams, Rowan. (2002). 'The Body's Grace'. In *Theology and Sexuality: Classic and Contemporary Readings,* edited by E. Rogers. Oxford: Blackwell: 309-21

Wilson, Philip B. (2006). *Being Single in the Church Today: Insights from History and Personal Stories*. Harrisburg, Pa.: Morehouse Pub.

Winner, Lauren F. (2005). *Real Sex: The Naked Truth About Chastity*. Grand Rapids, Mich.: Brazos Press.

Wold, Donald J. (1998). *Out of Order: Homosexuality in the Bible and the Ancient near East*. Grand Rapids, Mich.: Baker.

Yarhouse, Mark A. (2010). *Homosexuality and the Christian: A Guide for Parents, Pastors, and Friends*. Grand Rapids, Mich.: Baker.